Can You See The Rainbow?

The LAM Program:
Creating Limitless Possibilities for the Child with Special Needs

Love

Acceptance

Matters

Adrienne L. Murphy, MA CCC-SLP, RYT-200, Energy Practitioner
and
Lois A. Mettler, MA SciEd, RYT-200, Energy Practitioner

LAM Healing Arts, LLC

Can You See the Rainbow?
The LAM Program:
Creating Limitless Possibilities for the Child with Special Needs
Copyright © 2016 LAM Healing Arts, LLC

All rights reserved. No part of this book may be reproduced (except for inclusion in reviews), disseminated or utilized in any form or by any means, electronic or mechanical, including photocopying, recording, or in any information storage and retrieval system, or the Internet/World Wide Web without written permission from the author or publisher.

Book design by:
Arbor Books, Inc.
www.arborbooks.com

Printed in the United States of America

Can You See the Rainbow?
The LAM Program:
Creating Limitless Possibilities for the Child with Special Needs
Adrienne Murphy & Lois Mettler

1. Title 2. Author 3. Self-Help/Special Needs

Library of Congress Control Number: 2015919358

ISBN: 978-0-692-64248-1

Praise For
Can You See the Rainbow?

"The LAM Program for children with special needs is a cutting-edge, holistic and integrative therapy program that increases appropriate behaviors, positive social interaction, and the acceleration of developmental milestones in children with ADHD/ADD, Autism Spectrum Disorders (ASD), and genetic disorders. The LAM Program is unique in that it supports the loving relationship between the parent and the child while creating an innovative and mindful approach to handling challenging behavioral situations. It is truly a gift to be able to support this program."

Lawrence Rosen, MD,
Founder of the Whole Child Center

"The 21st century approach to being with your child is the LAM approach, that is, an affirmation of unconditional love with tools of engagement and play in a mindful and spirited manner that works for your child's individual needs! I love that you quote Louise Hay, one of my mentors in my own journey since 1984 when I discovered her! *What You Think of Me is None of My Business* was my go to book through the most difficult periods of my life. Bringing her back into our consciousness at this difficult transitional time on our tumultuous planet is so wise!"

Anna Villa-Bager,
Founder/Executive Director- MarbleJam Kids™®

"Adrienne Murphy and Lois Mettler have given parents and caregivers a genuine gift with the writing of *Can You See The Rainbow? The LAM Program: Creating Limitless Possibilities For The Child With Special Needs.* They speak with wisdom from years of experience, compassion and understanding as parents, and sincerity as practitioners that serve those with special needs. I am proud to know them as individuals and as colleagues. I am inspired by the way they have taken the intellect they possess as clinicians and embraced the need to practice more positive approaches to human interaction. LAM reminds parents to lovingly accept children for who they are and to celebrate the way they are designed. At times, some need permission to embrace uniqueness, live in the moment, and share those blessings with others."

Sarah Melone, P. T.
Founder/President- MarbleJam Kids™®

"Adrienne Murphy and Lois Mettler are women who speak from their true, authentic voice. The power of their sacred energy reaches out to all of us and inspires us to search, sit, and embrace our higher mind and deeper, true selves. To be in the presence of Adrienne and Lois and to experience their fully realized energy is to work in purity and light. They are now sharing their wisdom and creativity with the world and showing us a way to teach, heal and own our true selves. Breathe..."

Allyn Sitjar, RDT, LCAT
Director of Action Arts Center-Creative Arts Therapy,
Sparta, NJ & New York City

"As an occupational therapist that specializes in working with children with sensory processing disorders and their families, a huge part of my job is coaching parents as to how to identify sensory triggers to challenging behaviors and how to support their child in various environmental contexts based on their sensory needs. Adrienne and Lois speak to the concept of parental coaching and of 'supporting' the child rather than trying to 'fix' the child. This contemporary concept combined with their systematic synthesis of both eastern and western treatment approaches, coined the 'LAM Buffet' is groundbreaking. Finally, a detailed and mindful approach to help parents and professionals alike sort through and fuse the plethora of treatment techniques available to us to best meet the individual needs of the child/family."

Catherine Cavaliere, PhD, OTR/L
Sensory Smart Therapy Services

"With *Can You See the Rainbow?*, Adrienne and Lois capture the intimate aspects of spiritual training, emotional intelligence and self-development inherent in working with children with special needs. The LAM Program guides you to explore yourself: to rediscover the root of love you have for any child, while giving you the tools to share and communicate that love. It is that simple, yet far from easy. Thank you for completing this essential work."

Philip N. Lombardo, PT, DPT, SCS, CSCS, PES, CES, USATF
Physical Therapist at Paramus Orthopedic Physical Therapy
Vice President of Diamond Cutter Executive Team

"In a world where children are often pushed to fit into society's mold, it is refreshing to find the LAM approach that accepts the child as created, unique, and special. LAM's concept of 'supporting' versus 'fixing', inclusion of parents/caregivers as integral team members, as well as addressing their feelings of fear, anxiety, shame, and guilt are tenets that should be incorporated into any first-rate therapy program. LAM's holistic methodology and focus on creating a 'safe space' of unconditional love and acceptance fill in the gaps where other programs can fall short."

Andrea Moore, MA CCC-SLP
Owner, Beyond Expectations Speech Therapy

"The Coach Approach is seeing others as creative, resourceful and whole. Adrienne Murphy and Lois Mettler have taken a 'coach approach' to their work with special needs children, their parents and the professionals who care for them. The LAM approach creates a paradigm shift from fixing what's broken to supporting children's brilliance. The book is filled with case studies that bring their approach alive and testify to its efficacy. I highly recommend their approach."

Siobhan M. Murphy, Master Certified Coach

"Adrienne and Lois are the voice and hearts of the future for children with special needs. They approach children as whole and perfect and find the way into each child's unique gifts. May our world begin to see the beauty in what may not seem beautiful and may we deepen our listening to hear the cries of all children everywhere."

Sheryl Edsall
Director and Owner of Naturally Yoga, Glen Rock, NJ,
Ayruvedic Practitioner and Nutrition Specialist

"Breezed through the first few pages and I can already tell that this is a powerful book in a direction of bringing children into alignment with their calm, happy selves. We share exactly the same philosophy, in fact the story of the cracked pot is one I share at my yoga trainings for 'Yoga for the Differently-Abled Child'. Blessings on this adventure."

Allison Morgan MA, OTR, E-RYT
Creator of "Zensationalkids"

This book is dedicated to all children who are perfect, whole and complete just the way they are...

-Adrienne and Lois

Table of Contents

Foreward 1

Acknowledgements 3

Introduction 9

Chapter 1
The LAM Treatment Buffet 15

Chapter 2
LAM Energy Work 22

Chapter 3
The LAM Mindfulness Curriculum (Parent/Practitioner Training) 33

Chapter 4
Traditional Modalities Used In The LAM Program 51

Chapter 5
Non-Traditional Modalities Used in the LAM Program 65

Chapter 6
Specific LAM Strategies for Challenging Behavioral Situations 88

Chapter 7
Sample LAM Lesson Plans 103

Chapter 8
LAM'S Vision And Hope For The Future 133

Chapter 9
LAM's Offering of Inspirational Poems/Quotes/Affirmations 147

Endnotes 159

Foreword

A transformational journey that involves shifting the perception of both the parent and the professional from fixing to supporting the child with special needs

Adrienne L. Murphy, Master of Arts in Speech-Language Pathology and ASHA Certificate of Clinical Competence specializing in Early Intervention for children with special needs and Lois A. Mettler, Master of Science Education, professional puppet master and ACE Certified Personal Trainer excitedly joined forces to create the LAM Program for children with special needs. They originally met in 2011 at a Yoga Teacher Training program and earned their certifications as registered 200 Hour Yoga Alliance Teachers. Their playful natures and love for children forged their connection forever as kindred spirits during Children's Yoga Teacher Training. While teaching children's yoga at a local public school, they were involved with teaching children with special needs. During that time, with only twenty minutes of yoga, Adrienne and Lois witnessed profound change in the overall demeanor of these children. This is when their "AHA" moment led them to join paths. Their creative juices flowed at the prospect of adding additional Eastern therapeutic practices to their traditional Western professional backgrounds. Thus, began the pursuit of additional certifications in energy healing work.

LAM Energy healing work is the cornerstone of the LAM program. Parents and professionals can learn how to use this healing tool effectively with their special needs child in this book. Participants in the LAM Program have experienced first hand the depth of the LAM Energy work and learn its transformative applications while gaining the confidence for using this effective tool. This energy reduces the frequency and duration of meltdowns, crying episodes, and self-stimulating behaviors that have been documented consistently and observed by LAM professionals and parents of the children who have participated in the LAM Program. Children with special needs are especially vulnerable to environmental changes and very often don't feel safe. The transformative outcome of the LAM Energy work is the creation of a safe space quickly and effortlessly that is nurturing and grounding. From this anchor of safety, the child is able to grow and expand developmentally. In other words, traditional therapeutic outcomes can be achieved at a much faster rate with LAM energy work.

The addition of Eastern training practices inspired Adrienne and Lois to create the LAM Program, a cutting-edge 21st century program for children with special needs. LAM has become the natural name of this program because "LAM" is the seed sound in yoga philosophy that represents safety and security. LAM also stands for "Love, Acceptance Matters" which is a critical component of the LAM Program. Finally, quite surprisingly, LAM represents the initials of each of the co-founders' names.

With the cutting-edge holistic LAM therapeutic Program, parents and professionals will learn how to use certain strategies to integrate traditional Western therapeutic modalities with Eastern healing practices. This will create an accelerated achievement of developmental milestones for the child with special needs. The LAM Program also provides parents and professionals with much needed support and strategies for managing challenging behavioral situations. Finally, the "LAM Virtual Toolbox" can be applied in any situation at any time to alleviate family stress, power struggles and burnout. It requires a city to raise a child with special needs and the LAM Program is here to help do that!

Acknowledgements

This book is a labor of love. When we started our LAM Healing Arts Company in August 2013, we had a very specific vision. Our vision was to provide a fun-filled exciting and integrative program that would offer parents, professionals and children with special needs "limitless possibilities" and not "limitations." Thus, the name "LAM"- "Love, Acceptance Matters"- was born to join us together in our vision and to move it forward into a concrete manifestation of all that we believe personally and professionally.

We have to start by thanking each other for the amazing support and unconditional love we provided to each other during this journey. This journey not only consisted of clarity and purpose but also of ambiguity and uncertainty. Sometimes, there were clear landmarks for us to follow. Other times, the clouds rolled in and we had to have faith that we would see the rainbow again.

This book forced each of us to question our own beliefs and conditioned thought patterns. We realized that we, too, had to release our own "limitations" concerning the nature of this work in order to follow our vision and believe in its truth. When one of us had felt overwhelmed or unsure as to the nature of what we were doing, where we were going, or how we were going to do it, the other became the "anchor" or "grounding rod." Through this effortless flow of give and take, the work began to have a life and momentum of its own. We stopped questioning and just started surrendering and accepting this process, thus allowing faith and trust to guide us on this professional journey. In this manner, we "walked the talk" of the LAM program. Every concept we described in our book became the process for each of our own personal journeys as well. We were challenged every step of the way as we know all of our readers will be. We had to dig deep and find our own authentic selves in the very same manner that we described to you in this book. Looking back, we realize how necessary this process was. We are eternally grateful to be able to share this process with all of you.

Next, Adrienne would like to thank her family for their patience and love during this entire process. Adrienne would like to thank her beloved husband Peter, the love of her life. His support, love and devotion never once wavered during this entire process. Peter continued to offer Adrienne the encouragement to keep looking for the light when those cloudy days appeared. Adrienne would also like to thank her beloved son, Joe, for his openness and willingness to receive LAM Energy work and for his unconditional love and support. Joe has been his mom's greatest teacher. He has taught her about love, acceptance of the self and others, dedication, and following one's passion in life. Adrienne would like to thank her parents, Frank and Lori, for always supporting her in whatever new "path" she is pursuing. She would also like to thank her sister, Dani, for her excitement about the LAM program.

Lois would like to thank her supportive and loving husband, Gary, for understanding how important this work truly is and for giving up his office space frequently to put up with the chatter of this book writing process. Lois would like to thank Gary for readily accepting LAM Energy work unconditionally as a "test pilot." Lois would like to thank her daughter, Alyson, for being her inspiration about persistence, perseverance, focus and dedication. Thank you to her son, Gregg, for always lighting up any situation with humor and laughter. Thank you to Lois' siblings, Caroll and Jeff, for always believing in the validity of whatever path she was pursuing and always encouraging her to move forward. Thank you to Lois' friends for listening with an open mind to her passionate beliefs about the LAM program even though they wondered why she was doing all this work instead of retiring to Florida.

Finally, she would like to thank her parents who are alive in spirit guiding her although when physically alive, they had many reservations about spirituality.

A hearty thank you goes to Marble Jam Kids™®, the Creative Arts Therapy Center in River Edge, New Jersey for believing in the LAM program when it was in its gestation and infancy periods. We could have never given birth to the LAM program if it weren't for Marble Jam's support. Thank you to Anna Villa Bager and Sarah Melone for allowing us the opportunity to run our LAM Program at your center and wholeheartedly endorsing our program. When we first "pitched" our idea to Anna and Sarah, we had no idea as to the nature and structure of the LAM Program. LAM has enormous gratitude for Anna and Sarah who believed in the truth of the LAM vision and its programming. Thank you for allowing us to bring our ideas into manifestation supporting each change as it came. Lastly, thank you to all the Marble Jam families who participated in the LAM Program by taking a leap of faith and trusting in the LAM process.

A hearty thank you to Dr. Lawrence Rosen, MD, Founder of the Whole Child Center for believing in this work and viewing children as whole, perfect and complete. Complete gratitude to Allison Morgan, MA, OTR, E-RYT of "Zensational Kids" for all of your invaluable information and support of the LAM Program. David S. Evangelista, Disability and Development Expert, Board member Neitanaque, we wholeheartedly thank you for all of your time and support of our program. Emily Cobb, thank you for believing in LAM and for facilitating the connection to David Evangelista. Thank you to Dr. Matthew Holder, President of the American Academy of Developmental Medicine and Dentistry, for your amazing work with individuals with intellectual and developmental disabilities (IDD) and for endorsing our LAM program. Thank you to Dr. Phil Lombardo, PT, DPT, SCS, CSCS, PES, CES, USATF, Physical Therapist at Paramus Orthopedic Physical Therapy, Vice President of Diamond Cutter Executive Team who heartily endorsed our book upon meeting us and sharing common goals. Thank you to Allyn Sitjar, RDT, LCAT, Director of Action Arts Center-Creative Arts Therapy, Sparta,

NJ & New York City for all of your time, patience and expertise in sharing your creativity and wisdom with us. Thank you to Catherine Cavaliere, PhD., OTR/L, Director, Sensory Smart Therapy Services, Inc. for recognizing our "LAM Buffet" as "groundbreaking." Thank you to Andrea Moore, M.A. CCC-SLP, Owner, Beyond Expectations Speech Therapy for recognizing the importance of including parents/caregivers in the therapeutic process. A heart-felt thank you goes out to Siobhan M. Murphy, Master Certified Coach, who understands the importance of seeing each individual as "creative, resourceful and whole."

Thank you to all of Adrienne's speech pathology clients over the years. Without all of you, I never would have become the professional I am today.

Thank you to all of the many children Lois has taught and played with over the years as a high school science teacher and puppeteer. You have given her the greatest gift: how to play and find the way into the hearts and minds of children. Lois would not believe in "limitless possibilities" without all of you.

Thank you to LAM's first spiritual teachers, Sheryl and Neil Edsall of Naturally Yoga, a Bhakti yoga studio in Glen Rock, NJ. Lois and Adrienne first connected during their 200 Hour Yoga Teacher Training in September 2010 at Naturally Yoga. Adrienne and Lois love both Sheryl and Neil dearly for opening their hearts, minds and spirits to the sacred teachings of Yoga. Without this process, they would never have been able to connect to their authentic selves and realize their "dharma" (i.e. soul's purpose). The unconditional love and acceptance of Sheryl and Neil paved the way for them to transform and carry this knowledge forward into the LAM program. Thank you, Sheryl and Neil, for allowing Adrienne and Lois the opportunity to run one of their first "novel" energy healing workshops at the Naturally Yoga studio. Lastly, thank you Sheryl for endorsing our book and recognizing that LAM is "listening to hear the cries of all children everywhere."

Thank you to all the authors and spiritual teachers in the world. Some of you are already quoted in this book. Without your wisdom, the LAM path would have been much more difficult. A special thank you goes out to Oprah Winfrey and Deepak Chopra for the many Meditation Series that have inspired Adrienne and Lois over the last three years. These Meditation Series have been a source of wisdom, strength, clarity and peace for both of them. Special thank you to Tim Shriver for his book, *Fully Alive*, and for believing everyone is "fully alive" just as they are. Thank you, Tim, for believing in our LAM program. Thank you to Ron Suskind for your heart-felt book, *Life Animated*. So much of your own personal journey with your son has mirrored many of our own clients' journeys. You have given the world's children with special needs hope for a future filled with "limitless possibilities." Thank you to Louise Hay and Wayne Dyer for your wisdom and inspirational words. We miss you Wayne but know that you are always guiding LAM in spirit. Thank you to Lisa Rankin for integrating Eastern and Western medicine and inspiring us to do the same in the LAM program.

Lastly, thank you to all of the readers, parents and professionals who have chosen to learn about the LAM program and its application for children with special needs. It is LAM's hope that you will continue to find the rainbow in every day.

Introduction

"The whole world exists in love.
We come with love and we go with love.
And in between we live with love.
Love is the basis of everything."
(Sri Swami Satchidananda)[1]

This is our book of hope and support for all children who have special needs and the parents and professionals who work with them. As parents, we have walked in your shoes. But, as professionals, we have witnessed first-hand the amazing results of the LAM program. The LAM Program allows the parents and the professionals the opportunity to shift their beliefs about the challenges of the child with special needs from pessimism to optimism. This is analogous to seeing the rainbow of hope.

The slogan of "Love, Acceptance Matters" is the acronym for LAM. This book is an integration of both Eastern and Western healing philosophies. *The LAM Vision is to "Look at the child with special needs and envision the limitless possibilities not the limitations."* This **LAM Vision will create a New Paradigm for children with special needs: Change the perception from fixing the child to supporting the child. When this happens, it is LAM's Hope that LAM's ABC's of "A**cceptance of **L**imitless **P**ossibilities **B**ecomes **C**ommonplace" will become mainstream.** LAM truly does matter in this often chaotic and challenging world. It seems so simple yet it is so profound that parents are the captains of their child's ship. Professionals must never forget that parents must be included as part of the child's "support team." We are all partners in one big world ship.

The LAM paradigm focuses on the acceptance of a child at the particular developmental level he/she is displaying at any given moment. It shifts from "fixing" a child to "supporting" a child in whatever way is necessary to help the child to move forward developmentally, physically, emotionally and spiritually. As parents and professionals, we get caught up in the "checklists" which are used to determine the expectation of success for the child's development. By attaching to the "outcome" of what determines success in our society, we limit the possibilities for this child with special needs. Nothing illustrates this concept more clearly than this Chinese story by an anonymous writer:

"An elderly Chinese woman had two large pots, each hung on the ends of a pole which she carried across her neck. One of the pots had a crack in it while the other pot was perfect and always delivered a full portion of water. At the end of the long walks from the stream to the house, the cracked pot arrived only half full. For a full two years this went on daily, with the woman bringing home only one and a half pots of water. Of course, the perfect pot was proud of its accomplishments. But the poor cracked pot was ashamed of its own imperfection, and miserable that it could only do half of what it had been made to do. After two years of what it perceived to be bitter failure, it spoke to the woman one day by the stream. 'I am ashamed of myself, because this crack in my side causes water to leak out all the way back to your house.' The old woman smiled, 'Did you notice that there are flowers on your side of the path, but not on the other pot's side?' 'That's because I have always known about your flaw, so I planted flower seeds on your side of the path, and every day while we walk back, you water them.' For two years I have been able to pick these beautiful flowers to decorate the table. Without you being just the way you are, there would not be this beauty to grace the house'. Each of us has our own unique flaw. But it's the cracks and flaws we each have that make our lives together so very interesting and rewarding. You've just got to take each person for what they are and look for the good in them (Anonymous Author)."[2]

Our approach is very similar to this story. The LAM paradigm integrates Eastern and Western philosophies. As mentioned above, as a parent or professional, there is a tendency to limit expectations based on a developmental "checklist" that assumes all children develop in the same linear fashion. This is not the case. What might take two years for one child to achieve may take five years for another. The adages, "One size fits all" and " You aren't good enough" do not apply here at LAM.

We believe that a successful outcome will occur when one focuses his/her intention on the task at hand in a calm and loving manner and detaches from the outcome. This is the LAM approach. The child is seen as perfect, whole and complete instead of imperfect and in need of fixing. No child is ever compared to a universal standard or to other children. Every therapy used by LAM enables the whole beautiful child to emerge like a butterfly breaking free from the chrysalis. By changing the paradigm from "fixing" to "supporting", we are creating the necessary transformation in both the parent, professional and child that will lead to successful outcomes. Since the possibilities are limitless, any person who deals with the child must inherently believe that this truly is the case.

We have met many parents in our practice who display fear, shame and guilt over the child they have and who worry about their child's well-being and future adulthood. Some of the questions we have heard are just a few examples of the heart-breaking concerns of these parents: "Who will care for this child?" "Will this child ever be toilet-trained?" "Will this child ever understand directions and be compliant?" "Will this child ever talk?" "Will we ever be able to take this child out to a restaurant without a meltdown?" " Will this child ever go to college?" "Will this child ever "stop" while outside to cross a street?"

We have witnessed first-hand how our LAM therapy program has provided parents with hope, support, compassion and practical everyday strategies to navigate this complex course with their child. We believe that we all manifest our intentions on a daily basis. If you hope and dream big, these things will happen and yes you can have it all. And yes, "You can do it!" Thought becomes reality. We do create positive thoughts that in fact can change the world as we know it. As Gandhi once said, "Be the change you wish to see in the world."[3]

As LAM practitioners, we nurture and support the parent, professional and the child. We feel this is vital for the exchange of positive energy. Once we enhance this energy flow, everyone benefits and moves forward. Just as a seed needs the correct growing conditions of water, sun, and nutrients to develop magnificently, so does the relationship between the parent, professional and child with special needs.

It is our hope that this book will reach a wide audience of parents and professionals.

In order to change the paradigm from "fixing" to "supporting" the child with special needs, we at LAM foster creativity, happiness and harmony in parents, professionals and children. This creates the necessary safe space needed for all to flourish and to be their best selves.

The LAM Treatment Buffet

Traditional Therapies   *Non-Traditional Therapies*

Gross Motor · Play · Sensory · Speech · LAM Energy Work · Meditation · Yoga · Breath Work · Mindfulness · Qigong · Sound/Music

Safe Space

Chapter 1

The LAM Treatment Buffet

The Parent's Challenge

Parents imagine yourself on vacation at a fabulous buffet at an all-inclusive beach resort where the choices are endless, and for once you are not the chef. Delicious smells wafting into the air permeate your olfactory sense. There is pleasant music playing in the background as well as people conversing and waiters serving. You reflect, "This is going to be a fun-filled family vacation." You turn your gaze downward. Your special needs child is over-stimulated and holds his hands over his face. You don't know where to begin. You recognize the triggering of a meltdown simmering for your child. You become anxious. Your heart starts to pound. You start breaking a sweat. Your whole mood has changed from one of happiness to one of dread. You start at one end of the table with throngs of people waiting in line. You pause for a moment and view the delectable array of bountiful edibles. You feel overwhelmed by the dizzying array of choices and people in your immediate surroundings. Your child is now tugging at you, crying and screaming loudly enough to grab everyone's attention. The dreaded meltdown has begun with no help in sight. Your spouse or significant other is nowhere to be found. Your body tenses, your stomach hurts, and your headaches. You want to grab your child and run out of there and go to a safe space where people don't look at you like you're a "bad parent" and look at your child as if he is a "monster."

What do you do? Do you run out of there resentful and bitter that your child has once again "ruined" another pleasurable experience for you? If you stay, the tension will escalate and your child will reach his breaking point of no return. So, you retreat dragging your child hard by the hand as two warriors in battle not only against the world but also with each other. You both are heart-broken. There are no winners in this battle. There are no weapons to sustain this battle. You are both defeated.

It doesn't have to be this way. LAM is here to help you navigate this buffet. At the "LAM Buffet", you can sigh with relief and relax knowing that you will have a "fun-filled family vacation". The buffet table is one-of-a-kind. It is a symbolic table that represents all of the various "tools" that we at LAM can offer you for a wonderful experience. This buffet will nourish both you and your child and will give you the pleasure of choice in this process. You will become the "Guide" in the experience that your child lovingly accepts without resistance. Your child will become an active participant with controlled choices.

The Professional's Challenge

Professionals, we are certain that you too have witnessed a child's challenging behaviors during your sessions with children with special needs. Have you felt stressed during these challenging moments? Have you ever felt that you accomplished nothing in a session? The "LAM Buffet" is an additional "tool" to use in conjunction with your traditional practice. It is LAM's belief that the "LAM Buffet" will enhance your professional experience by reducing professional burnout and helping you achieve more positive outcomes for yourself, the child and his/her family.

So, let's set our LAM Buffet for both parents and professionals…

First, please pick the buffet table with care and set it for the most important holiday with special china, silver, flowers, candles and crystal, etc. Anyone invited to this holiday table will feel the beauty, warmth, love, peace and joy of experiencing it. The LAM buffet table is the safest space you can create in order for joy and happiness to abound.

All must feel happy, supported, nurtured and peaceful in this space. It is the sacred space upon which the LAM choices are made.

Second, please take a LAM plate. These plates are set up in the middle of every LAM buffet table. Every plate at this buffet table contains LAM Energy work. It is the intuitive exchange of the energy of love and acceptance that creates positive interaction and support. We will provide extensive details on LAM Energy work in Chapter Two. You will learn and feel comfortable in using these "tools" to tap into your own energy and intuition in order to create this beautiful plate.

Third, you will need to choose which "foods" will nourish everyone. Here are your "food choices". On the left end of the table are the more "traditional" therapies such as gross motor, play, sensory and speech. On the right end of the table are the more "non-traditional therapies" of meditation, breath work, yoga, mindfulness, Qigong and sound/music. The combinations are endless. Don't be overwhelmed by the wide array of choices. All you have to do is choose one from the left and one from the right and put it on your plate. How will you decide? The LAM Program will help you make the correct choice.

Parents and professionals, we will be your guides and empower you to use these LAM tools in an effortless way that will become second nature to you. A sense of calm, focus, and relaxation will occur when you are working with the child. You will be able to observe challenging behaviors instead of reacting to them all the time. As a parent, you will be able to enjoy your child and be able to play with him/her. As a professional, you will be able to move this child forward developmentally in an accelerated manner. These extraordinary changes will ripple positivity and light to both the family and to the community.

Whether you are a parent or a professional, these changes may seem slow since you must excavate and uncover your own negative thought and emotional patterns and release them. All human beings possess limiting cultural conditioning, hidden fears, and anxieties. Therefore, it is not a surprise that most of us react in predetermined ways to the child's behaviors. You have to be willing to take the necessary steps to change your own negative patterns so that you are able to witness the child's behaviors instead of reacting to them. This will be discussed in detail in Chapter Three: The LAM Mindfulness Curriculum (Parent/Professional Training).

So, by now you are probably thinking to yourself, "Why should I do this LAM Program? Where is the efficacy data?" Both of the LAM co-creators have been trained as "western professionals" with master's degree training in speech pathology and science education. We were skeptics like you at the beginning of this LAM process. But, something inside of us always searched for more answers beyond what we could see and touch in only the physical world. We wanted to see the rainbow in each and every child with special needs. We sought answers in Eastern Healing philosophies and practices. We started to blend these practices in our own "traditional Western" approach and witnessed firsthand dramatic changes in our clients and their parents. There was no holding us back. Our unbridled passion for this work was the impetus behind the creation of our LAM Healing Arts, LLC business. Working at a Creative Arts Therapy Center, "MarbleJam Kids™®" in Bergen County, NJ enabled us to create LAM programs that would treat a wide variety of children with special needs in this new holistic manner. East met west and the rest is history.

The names of our case studies have been changed to protect the privacy and identity of our clients. As LAM practitioners, we detach from the outcome but are heavily invested in the process with detailed goals and objectives for every child.

CASE STUDY NUMBER ONE- KEVIN D. AND BETTY (MOM)

Kevin D. was an eight-year-old boy diagnosed with Down Syndrome when we first met him. He was a veteran of the traditional therapeutic process from birth. When we met him, he was not fully toilet trained. Kevin's mom, Betty, expressed to us how hard it was for her to change and diaper an eight year old but she was filled with hope. His developmental age was about four years in receptive/expressive language skills, social skills and overall cognitive ability. Kevin displayed poor eye contact and poor focus for any structured play task. He exhibited low frustration tolerance for new or harder tasks. He had a hard time with transitions. Gross and fine motor skills were severely delayed with fine motor skills being the most impaired. Kevin loved music and movement in his body. He was hypotonic in his overall musculature and oral tone. He had a poor attention span but his mood was compliant. Kevin's mom reported frequent meltdown episodes of crying at home. Mom seemed very emotionally grounded at the beginning of treatment. She was loving and accepting of Kevin and really wanted to see him make progress. Kevin's mom was playful and easily followed our guidance with regards to use of specific LAM strategies. Mom was willing to participate in our "Mindfulness Curriculum" that will be discussed in detail in Chapter Three.

Our "LAM Treatment Buffet" had many options for Kevin. First, we created our LAM Buffet Table or "safe space" through the use of music, gentle movement, and smiles with the intention of facilitating playful interaction between Kevin and his mom. Once established, we added the "plate" of LAM Energy work that will be discussed in detail in Chapter Two. We then added the traditional "foods" of "play therapy", "speech therapy" and "sensory therapy" which will be discussed in detail in Chapter Four. Then, we added the "non-traditional foods" of yoga movement, breathwork, sound therapy, mantra and relaxation. These modalities will be discussed in detail in Chapter Five.

Kevin responded extremely well to our LAM treatment plan. We worked with him for about six months once a week. The developmental and behavioral changes we saw were astounding! Kevin exhibited greater attention, compliance and transition skills. He easily relaxed with the LAM Energy work and followed all directions well. He initiated conversation and had more spontaneous expressive language without prompts. He became more social. He blurted out a lot, "I love yoga!" and " I love you mom." He became our "group leader" for the sound therapy portion of our class. Mom was thrilled because she reported, "Finally he was going to the bathroom on his own!" Kevin's mom described the changes in her son as a "dramatic improvement."

Looking back at Kevin's progress, one can observe that he benefited greatly from the LAM Treatment program. He then was discharged from our program to a more traditional creative arts therapy program in music. Months later, Kevin's mom would tell the LAM practitioners that Kevin expressed the desire to have "more yoga." The LAM program incorporates yoga, but to Kevin it seemed as if yoga and the holistic practices were paramount to the traditional modalities. We concluded that the combination of the different modalities used with the LAM energy work created a new sense of peace and joy in Kevin.

That's the beauty and success of the LAM program. It synergizes all the modalities to create a "fabulous buffet." Now, let's go back to the vacation buffet we originally set up at the beginning of this chapter and see how the LAM program would have changed the outcome for both the parent and child. In addition, let's see how the "LAM Buffet" can enhance one's professional practice.

First, the LAM parent would be totally mindful of his/her child being upset at the sensory stimuli present in that environment. As much as the original parent was excited at the prospect of enjoying this fabulous vacation, the LAM parent now would have the awareness that his/her child was not feeling safe in that situation. The LAM parent would not be exercising control over the child, but rather would be reading the child's cues. The LAM parent would realize that his/her child needed loving support and safety in such a stressful environment. Recognizing that this situation might create a negative reaction from the child, the LAM parent would seek to create a safe space before the meltdown would occur. Perhaps, the safe space would be away from all the activity. Or the child could sit alone with the LAM parent in a less stimulating environment. Another option for the LAM parent would be to introduce the child to the buffet earlier in the day without all the people present. In any event, the LAM parent would be able to anticipate the needs of his/her child in a compassionate way sharing the responsibility of the child's special needs. In this manner, the LAM parent would become the guide and the support for the child rather than the controller. Subtle changes do make a substantial difference here. The energy transfer between parent and child would be one of loving acceptance vs. controlling dominance. In this LAM paradigm, the child would become acquiescent instead of resistant. Feeling bathed in the warmth of support from the parent, the child would not feel fearful or anxious while navigating his external world. Compassion, love and understanding would be the critical operating principles here instead of force, domination and control.

Second, the LAM professional would stay solely focused in the present moment in a calm and compassionate manner. No matter whether the outcome is positive or negative, the professional wouldn't feel professional success or failure. Instead, the professional would know that he/she had provided the best level of care possible with love and compassion. This would assuage any self-blame or self-criticism the professional might attach to the outcome. The result of this change in philosophy would facilitate less stress and burnout for the professional.

Now, parents and professionals, let's break down this LAM Buffet into various sections in the forthcoming chapters to explain in detail each element. From these explanations, we guarantee that you will feel comfortable and at ease using this buffet in any situation that may arise. Fasten your seatbelts and get ready to open your mind, heart and spirit for a journey that will take you to uncharted terrain. All we ask is that you are open to receive this information without judgment or expectation about the outcome. Remember that you are sampling a buffet where you are able to choose carefully what is right for you to take and use. You do not have to sample everything on the table. Here we go…

Chapter 2

LAM Energy Work

What is "LAM Energy Work?" Does this sound "out there" or "far-fetched" like something from outer space? Let's start with the definitions of energy.

What is energy? According to Webster's dictionary, "energy" is defined as "the capacity for work or vigorous activity."[4] Another definition of energy is Albert Einstein's Theory of Relativity that states: "Energy equals mass times the velocity of light squared."[5] A third definition of energy is that it is "Nature's set of building blocks, out of which she constructs every material thing in the universe, including humankind, and every form of animal and vegetable life. Through a process that only Nature completely understands, she translates energy into matter."[6] In other words, energy is defined as what it does for or to you rather than what it truly is. Energy has no form/substance unless it is doing something. For example, there are many different forms/types of energy that we can see and feel in our everyday lives: heat, electrical, chemical, etc. So, as humans we can feel energy in these various forms. You can burn yourself, feel a static shock, and see chemical reactions to various cleaning substances on your body such as rashes. Clearly, these are examples of energy in concentrated form that is felt by humans.

Let's delve into the subtlety of energy that we can't see, feel, or touch but that we know exists. Some examples are: the energy that cooks your food in a microwave, X rays of your body that tell you if you have any broken bones, MRIs to detect tumors etc. On a lighter side, everyday examples of energy could include the use of your TV, car, cell phone and

WiFi connection. How does that work? We can't see or feel that energy per se but we certainly know when it is not present. For example, when you lose the energy that makes your car run, or you lose your Internet and cell phone connections, you feel disconnected from the world and your stress energy rises.

Let's go into an even more subtle expression of energy that you probably experience in your life. What is subtle energy? Subtle energy is the energy you feel from different people when you walk in a room and can just "sense" that something is either good, bad or OK. Not a word is usually said about this but you can certainly feel it. For example, as a parent of a special needs child, you may feel the energy of tension surrounding you at an IEP meeting. Other examples are that you may even say to yourself, " I got a good vibe from that person I met tonight at the party" or " I felt that they didn't want me around." Some of these feelings could be due to your perception but a majority of it is directly due to your "sensing" or "reading" the energy flow between you and another person. You use this "sense" of knowing in all aspects of your daily life. Why not use this subtle energy with your own child and family?

The Law of Attraction is defined as "the energy that you put out into the world is returned to you in kind."[7] Sir Isaac Newton defined this occurrence in his Third Law of Motion in Physics which states, "For every action, there is an equal and opposite reaction."[8] In LAM Energy work, what this means is that your intention about the child either as the parent or professional creates the reality for both you and the child. If you align with the child's energy as an ally or supporter, you co-create an exchange of energy that vibrates love and acceptance. Oprah Winfrey says, "…the energy we send out is also being returned to us. Oprah calls this phenomenon, 'Universal Law' that guides us just as it guides the planets. Change your energy and you can change your entire experience in the world. Change your intention and you can change your path. Our intentions create our words, our thoughts, our actions, and our experiences." [9] Many spiritual teachers refer to this phenomenon as "The Law of Attraction." LAM believes that this law accurately describes how energy is transferred between the parent, professional and child.

So, it makes sense to reason that if parents send out the vibrations of fear, anger, shame, and guilt, the child will return those vibrations in kind. If the professional sends out vibrations of "fixing " a "broken" child instead of "supporting" a child that is already "whole" and "complete," the child will return those vibrations to the professional and feel weak and helpless. However, if you choose to accept the child as is and change your energetic vibrations to love, joy, peace, and compassion, the child will respond to you accordingly. It is amazing to think that you can choose this new LAM paradigm by simply changing your intention and being present with the child in a loving and peaceful manner. This will create a positive dyad or coupling that supports instead of resists. This is the LAM Energy transfer that is so transformational.

CASE STUDY NUMBER TWO:
KAREN S. AND BARBARA (MOM)

A case study illustrating this principle is Karen S. and her mother Barbara. Karen was an eighteen-month-old girl diagnosed with a genetic abnormality, gross developmental delays and hypotonia in core, upper extremities and in oral motor musculature. This child could barely hold her head and trunk erect when we first met her. She lacked age-appropriate feeding skills and only drank from a bottle. She was non-verbal and unable to communicate her wants and needs consistently. She did not demonstrate a consistent pointing gesture and lacked the ability to crawl or roll over. Socially, she exhibited anxiety if physically someone got too close to her as evidenced by her pushing the person away and grinding her teeth with an angry look on her face. Mom was extremely consumed with finding the right "fix" or "therapies" to help her daughter. Karen received physical therapy (PT), occupational therapy (OT) and speech therapy (ST) as well hydrotherapy and nutritional therapy. This child was exhausted from all of these therapy sessions. Her mom spent the majority of her time "searching" for new therapies on the Internet while a nanny interacted with her daughter.

First and foremost, the LAM practitioners had to create a safe space for this child and her mom. We met the child at her unique developmental level and engaged her with toys in order to elicit a fundamental desire to communicate through eye contact and hand reaching. The LAM practitioners involved mom right away in the play session and told her to carve out special time each day to interact and play with her daughter. The "LAM intention" was to create a peaceful and nurturing space where Karen and her mom felt connected and playful. Non-judgment and acceptance of both Karen and her mom at that particular moment in time as perfect, whole and complete were the LAM guiding principles. There was no expectation about outcome. They both relaxed into the unconditional love and acceptance of the moment. Once the LAM practitioners created the safe space, the LAM Energy work began. The LAM practitioners used the specific intention of eliciting physical and neurological changes in Karen's body during the energy work. This LAM energy work consisted of using that specific intention to energize Karen's body and to create new neural pathways and bridges for speech-language development and motor planning. This energy work also involved the release of any negative blocks or patterns that were inhibiting energy flow. Karen responded rapidly to this treatment.

In one session, she was able to engage in reciprocal vocalization and attempted to move her hands in imitation during finger play songs. She attempted the hand gesture sign for "more" and bent her knees in the supine position with feet flat on floor moving hips from adduction to abduction. Mom was thrilled with this progress and came to us with Karen for 15 additional sessions at which time we discharged her. During this course of treatment, mom reduced the frequency of Karen's other traditional therapies to allow her daughter's body to rest, heal, and absorb the energy work. Mom learned how to play effectively and lovingly with her daughter through our guidance. Mom and Dad attended our Mindfulness Curriculum Workshop in order to relax and meet their daughter at a higher vibrational level of love and acceptance rather than at a lower vibrational level of fear and worry. Mom also received two private LAM energy sessions and Dad received one that helped to clear their negative belief patterns. Miraculously, over the next nine months, Karen made tremendous strides over the course of sixteen sessions.

Improvements were observed in all areas of her development: gross motor, fine motor, speech and behavior. She could now stand and take a few steps with minimal assistance. She was vocalizing and using a few word approximations to express her wants and needs. She was moving her mouth appropriately and eating a wider variety of foods. She was more social with the LAM practitioners and mom. Eye contact was appropriate. Her communicative intent was to engage with the surrounding adults. During the last two sessions, we instructed mom in the use of "LAM intention" to continue to facilitate Karen's social, emotional and physical development. Mom was reluctant to do this and felt anxious that she would make a mistake. We told her that by just being clear and intending love and acceptance to Karen, she could not do any harm. Mom courageously trusted our advice and moved forward.

Today, Karen is thriving. Mom reported to us that Karen is "fantastic" and continuing to make steady progress in all developmental areas. As mom's conscious awareness evolved, she changed her paradigm and started to believe in herself and her intuition. Mom used clear intentions to facilitate change in all members of her family. She clearly became the catalyst for transformation. It is not a surprise that this case study is a LAM success story.

How can the parent or professional use intention to help the child with special needs progress in all areas of his/her life?

What really is "intention?" The Free Merriam-Webster Dictionary defines intention as "a thing intended; an aim or plan."[10] Another definition is: "an act or instance of determining mentally upon some action or result."[11] In LAM Energy work, the parent or professional uses positive intentions to create harmony between themselves and the child. This leads to the creation of safety, security and happiness. As the parent or professional, you can focus your attention on love and acceptance in any situation with the child. Having an intention and then letting go of the outcome is the LAM secret to the attainment of the child's true potential. When you are open to believing and accepting whatever the outcome with the child will be, you will be able to guide the child to the next positive step in his/her journey. This will facilitate a positive exchange of energy between you and the child.

In the Western world, traditional therapy and parenting are all based on "developmental checklists." There is very little wiggle room here to meet the child in his/her space at his/her level. Many times, one often misses seeing the subtleties and gifts of every child. Parents and professionals are "trained" to believe that reaching desired goals is the only way to measure a child's success. This intention is all well and good. However, we all know that all children develop in their own unique way. For children with special needs, this is especially true in the "scattering" of skills you may see on a particular test or re-evaluation. Rigid expectations and goals often do not allow for the acceptance of any other outcome. Parents and professionals are even surprised if a child moves forward in an unexpected way. This phenomenon of a child moving forward unexpectedly was exhibited by another one of our LAM children.

CASE STUDY NUMBER THREE:
MIKE A. AND GABRIELLA (MOM)

After nine months of working with Mike A, we trained Gabriella, Mike's mom, in the use of positive intention to create the safe space of love, peace and nurturing for her child. Mom used this practice about four times a week at bedtime when alone with her child. After a month of using this practice, one of the occupational therapists at this child's school stopped to ask the mom, "What have you been doing differently with your son? He has met all of my treatment goals in the last month." The therapist seemed baffled by this and had no explanation for the sudden gains this child had made.

Could it be this simple? Does love and acceptance matter more than practicing particular skills? This is the power of positive intention.

It cannot be under-estimated.

To clarify, let's take our hypothesis to another level. In Ron Suskind's book, *Life Animated*, he described how his family revolved around the needs of Owen, his younger son with autism while Walt, his older son, was highly successful in all areas of his life. The energy between Walt and his parents was enormously positive. Neither parent was worried about this child and his abilities to move forward in the world. The intentions of love and joy flowed freely back and forth between this older child and his parents. Unconsciously, the parents were using positive intention to promote this older child's journey to explore the world and its limitless possibilities. Positive intention equals positive results. This child flourished into a magnificent adult.

Ron Suskind's younger child, Owen, experienced regressive autism before the age of three. Before the autism diagnosis, Owen was described by his father as a "normal" two and a-half-year-old boy. Then, all of a sudden, Owen's new skills (speech, gross motor, fine motor, play and social interaction) rapidly disappeared. Ron Suskind stated, "The boy vanished."[12]

Initially, Ron Suskind and his wife were in denial and were ashamed of the diagnosis of autism. Then, after they accepted the diagnosis, they experienced anxiety and fear for their child's development and worried about his future. This put them on a "therapy wheel" to try to make this child move forward. During this time, Owen made very limited gains. He was unreachable. The parents experienced isolation from peers and focused all their attention and energy on Owen. They used all of their resources to create a team of therapists and nothing penetrated.

It is LAM's belief that the energy surrounding this child was one of negativity due to the prevalence of despair, shame, grief and fear. These negative unconscious feelings or in LAM terms "low energetic vibrations" were being felt by their child with autism. This resulted in the child not being able to move forward appropriately even with all the therapy in place. Miraculously, something happened to change this paradigm. What was it?

According to Ron Suskind, his son, Owen loved Disney characters and videos before the diagnosis. The entire family would watch Disney videos and they were a source of great pleasure before the diagnosis. Ron states that these videos were "something parents and kids could do together, and always within reach…when Owen arrived, he slotted right in with Walt. It was the house he was born into."[13]

After the diagnosis, Owen received a multitude of therapies. When he was exhausted at the end of his day, his mom would allow him to watch Disney videos. The parents were concerned that he was constantly rewinding certain videos and watching the same scenes over and over. They consulted with the professionals who assured them that if this activity kept him "relaxed" and "joyful," the parents "should just limit his viewing but not eliminate it entirely."[14]

Despite the Western therapeutic view that Owen's love of Disney characters was perseverative, it is LAM's belief that this love and almost "obsession" with these characters created the safe space for the family to bond and connect on a truly authentic level. This safe space allowed Owen the opportunity to be his true self. It is no surprise to LAM that this was the breakthrough into Owen's inner world. Ron describes this breakthrough moment when Owen kept repeating the "gibberish"… "juicervose, juicervose." The family finally determined that Owen had the motivational intent to communicate with his family and was really saying, "Just your voice"! The entire family was overjoyed and joined together with Owen bouncing, laughing and singing while mom whispered, "Thank God… he's in there."[15]

Meeting this child in his sacred space, the parents encouraged all the therapists to create treatment plans with Disney characters/videos to meet this child where he was. Next, instead of worrying all the time, the parents and therapists felt more hopeful. They played with Owen in his Disney world. As soon as this occurred, the parents' and therapists' intentions of despair and worry changed to possibility, hope and joy. This famous case study illustrates clearly the LAM paradigm of "love, acceptance matters."

We conclude that the intention for this or any other child with special needs must be one of joy, happiness, love and acceptance. Fear, worry, despair, shame, and grief must not enter into your intentions. Children with special needs have special abilities to intuit what you truly feel about them. They require parents and professionals who are optimistic, patient, level headed, compassionate, tolerant and hopeful. This is not an easy task when the child is exhibiting severe symptoms such as meltdowns, screaming and resistant behaviors. It requires courage, strength and trust that whatever will be, will be. We must detach from the outcome and trust in the process with our heartfelt intentions. By doing this, you are guaranteeing the best possible outcome for the child. This may not look like true success as viewed by the Western world, but everyone will be happy, content and peaceful. We will discuss in greater detail how you can transform your intentions to peace, love and joy. We will also demonstrate to you how you can clear negative belief patterns in Chapter Three: The LAM Mindfulness Curriculum (Parent/Professional Training).

Intention is the cornerstone of LAM Energy work. In layman's terms, in order to have water first flow out of your faucet, you must first "intend" to turn the faucet on. In order to turn on a light in a room, you must "intend" to turn "on" the switch. If your intention is powerful and strong, you will turn on the water or flip the switch. So, if you "intend" strongly enough, change will happen. In energy language, we create change with an intention that manifests in an outcome. Our premise for LAM Energy Work is for parents and professionals to create an "intention" that is so focused and conscious that it will create a positive outcome.

LAM energy work is a "healing tool" that goes deep into the body, mind, and spirit through focused "intention." It transforms emotions, negative belief patterns, and physical behaviors. It grounds, centers, and nurtures those who receive its energy. Since it harnesses frenetic energy, this is especially effective for children with special needs. This energy reduces the frequency and duration of meltdowns, crying episodes, and self-stimulating behaviors that have been documented consistently and observed by LAM professionals and parents of the children who have participated in the LAM program. This energy improves eye contact, ease of transitioning, socialization, pretend play, and receptive and expressive language skills. The remarkable results are that the relationship among the parent, child and professional deepens. In addition, both the parent and professional are empowered when dealing with challenging situations. In other words, a flow of positive high vibrational energy occurs in everyone. This will lead to a reduction of frustration in the parent and of burnout in the professional.

CASE STUDY NUMBER FOUR:
ANDREW H. AND FAYE (MOM)

Faye initially came to one of our "LAM Informational Sessions" crying to us about her son Andrew who was nine years old. She said he was in overall good health now but had suffered a stroke at one week old in the NICU. He had had some prenatal issues and currently exhibited many food sensitivities/allergies in blood work. She reported that he was bullied in school, very sensitive to his peers and at times suffered from social isolation. He had difficulty learning due to attention issues and was prone to behavioral outbursts of anger at home. He suffered from anxiety as evidenced by panic attacks due to the fear of being alone and in the dark. Mom reported that at times he still slept in her bed. Andrew attended a regular public school and was mainstreamed. He had an aide in his classroom. At our first session, Andrew was extremely quiet but compliant. Eye contact was poor when interacting with the LAM practitioners. He seemed anxious and fearful. He exhibited poor emotional affect during play. He exhibited all appropriate responses for structured speech-language and cognitive tasks that were presented to him. He participated in non-traditional tasks such as breathwork and yoga movement. At that time, he reacted most strongly to puppet play. He also exhibited strong emotions when he shared his love of art.

Following the LAM Treatment Buffet model, the LAM practitioners created a safe space by joining Andrew H. and his mom in puppetry play. LAM energy work was used during this first session to relax mom and Andrew and to create a bond based on mutual love and acceptance. Over the course of the next three sessions, Andrew brought in samples of his artwork and began to show more emotional affect while sharing his artwork. During that time period, Mom engaged in our Mindfulness Curriculum Workshop and had a private session with the LAM practitioners. At the fourth session, Andrew and his mom were discharged. Since that time, mom and Andrew have enjoyed a more positive and peaceful relationship. At a later time, Faye happily reported that Andrew was no longer exhibiting any of his original symptoms. School was going smoothly and peer relationships were occurring.

In this particular case, it is LAM's belief that the most important thing to remember is the power of the mom's intention and its impact on her son's development. Originally, Faye, Andrew's mom, held the unconscious intentions of fear, guilt and shame toward herself and son. LAM believes that these unconscious intentions manifested as the negative behavior patterns her son was exhibiting in his everyday life. The source of these negative unconscious intentions stemmed from the difficulties she had experienced with her son as an infant. Mom blamed herself for all of these difficulties and passed on this negative energy to her son. After her participation in the LAM program, she was able to let go and release these negative belief patterns. Her intentions for both herself and her son changed dramatically from fear, shame and guilt to those of acceptance, love and joy. Her son, in turn, picked up this positive energy and began to experience a radical positive transformation.

In conclusion, LAM Energy work uses focused intention to create "the perfect meal" at the LAM Buffet. Remember, LAM Energy work cannot be seen. **LAM Energy work is FELT by all who practice and receive it.** It is a very powerful tool to use. It must be practiced frequently and consistently with focused intention. The LAM Mindfulness Curriculum is essential for learning and using LAM Energy work. Let's move on to Chapter Three to study and learn the LAM Mindfulness Curriculum in greater detail.

Chapter 3

The LAM Mindfulness Curriculum (Parent/Practitioner Training)

"Every night I work with Mike using the techniques you taught me. We continue to see gains in language and overall connection to the world around him."
(Gabriella B., mother of Mike age 5)

We at LAM feel that understanding the LAM Mindfulness Curriculum is critical for parents and professionals who work with this population of children. The LAM Mindfulness Curriculum is the cornerstone of our LAM work. Parents and professionals are particularly susceptible to stress and over-reactivity since they are always on "high alert" with special needs children. The burnout rate for professionals who work with this population is staggering. Parents live in a "fight or flight" response and activate the sympathetic nervous system continually. They are living on the edge facing unknown territory with professionals, peers and family. Everyone outside is looking in and judging whether or not the particular situation is being handled "correctly." Parents, you might be even judging yourself or your spouse all the time. As a parent, you think you "should" be doing something better or different to "fix" your child.

An example of a parent's dilemma is seeing one professional and receiving the opinion that you need the advice of another "professional" for your particular case. As a parent, you meet with this new "professional" and don't receive any real answers. As a result, parents keep moving from one professional to the next. All of these differing diagnoses lead to confusion and the loss of connection to a parent's inner voice of knowing. This may lead to all sorts of division among family members and spouses because the vibrational energy of the family now consists of confusion, fear, shame, depression, worthlessness, and anxiety.

It is no surprise that the divorce rate for parents of children with special needs is higher than the national average of 50 percent. The demands of caring for siblings, full-time jobs, and negative behavioral issues may create an unstable family life where the higher energetic vibrations of compassion, love, peace and joy seem unattainable. We at LAM know that these challenges are enormous! Expectations for a happy and peaceful marriage and family life may seem to be out of reach.

As a professional, one is typically seeing the child on average one to two times per week for hourly sessions Professionals may be at a loss as to how to help each family navigate the stressors effectively. Professionals are encumbered by insurance companies, paperwork and reduced actual time for patient care. Usually, a third party monitors professionals closely so that certain standards and developmental goals are achieved in a timely manner. Professionals often feel very stressed by this and experience a high rate of professional burnout and frustration. This is the precise reason why the LAM program was developed: to meet the unique needs of the parent and child with special needs, the family and the professional.

So, what can be done to change "the system?" **The LAM MINDFULNESS CURRICULUM COMES TO THE RESCUE!**

The LAM Mindfulness Curriculum offers both parents and professionals the strategies to cope and manage their stressful lives in a more constructive proactive way where one becomes "conscious" and less reactive. This chapter teaches you how to co-create an environment of peace and love for the child. Instead of being reactive, you become the "observer" and "guide" for the child. The child feeds off of this higher vibrational energy of unconditional love and acceptance. Instead of being reactive, you become a coach lovingly moving the child forward in a positive manner. This is a process that takes time and doesn't happen overnight. This process involves deep introspection and the willingness to move from your ego to your authentic self. So, what is the difference between the ego and the authentic or true self?

WHAT IS THE EGO?

We at LAM define the ego as your "Illusionist Self." This is the self that you have been conditioned to "present" to the world. This "Illusionist Self" or "Ego" pretends to be someone that you may or may not want to be but thinks that you "should be" given your upbringing and belief systems. The external world creates certain standards that dictate how one should feel, look or behave. Wealth, beauty, achievements, and professional accomplishments drive the ego. If something in our life doesn't "show" well, our ego gets upset. As a result, our ego feels anger, shame, resentment and worthlessness.

Deepak Chopra states on his website, "The ego is our self-image, not our true self. It is characterized by labels, masks, images, and judgments."[16] Dr. Phil speaks of the ego as the "fictional self" and says on his website, "When you live a life that has you ignoring your true gifts and talents while performing assigned or inherited roles instead, you are living as your fictional self. You may have found that it's easier to fill the roles your family and friends expect of you, rather than becoming who you really want to be. Living this way drains you of the critical life energy you need to pursue the things you truly value. The fictional self sends you false information about who you are and what you should be doing with your life. It blocks the information you need in order to maintain the connection with your authentic identity. Relying on information from the fictional self means you're putting your trust in a broken compass."[17]

We at LAM believe that you will become adversarial to the child if you live in your ego. Parents may experience resentment, anger, fear, frustration and shame since their child may not live up to their ego's expectations. Professionals may feel frustrated and burned out since the child may not be progressing in a timely manner. Professionals may receive negative feedback from the parents who are anxious and angry when they don't see gains in developmental milestones. Professionals often feel upset and unappreciated when they aren't able "to fix" a child with their particular expertise.

As we all know, children with special needs typically do not "show well" in many situations. As a parent and professional, if you judge yourself based on the child's performance all the time, you may feel disappointment in the outcomes. This is your "ego" speaking. The "ego" has taken charge of this situation and is running the "show." In turn, the child picks up the lower energetic vibration of the ego and may feel unaccepted, unsupported and unloved. This will create an environment that lacks the safe space that is so necessary for the child to grow and flourish. This is precisely why the creation of the safe space at the "LAM Buffet" is the first step in changing "the system" that is so vital to moving the child forward. The LAM Mindfulness Curriculum teaches the parent/professional how to move out of one's ego and into one's authentic/true self so that a safe space can be created. This understanding of the ego and authentic/true self is the first step in the LAM Mindfulness Curriculum training.

WHAT IS YOUR AUTHENTIC/TRUE SELF?

There have been many definitions of the authentic self in both psychology and philosophy. Dr. Phil states on his website that "the authentic self is the you that can be found at your absolute core. It is the part of you not defined by your job, function or role. It is the composite of all your skills, talents and wisdom. It is all of the things that are uniquely yours and need expression, rather than what you believe you are supposed to be and do."[18]

In yoga and Eastern Philosophy, the authentic self is often defined as the Soul, True Self, Higher Self, Inner Guru, Piece of Divinity or the God that lives within you as you. It is your absolute essence. It is never affected by thought patterns such as "should/would/could." Circumstances, belief patterns and conditioning patterns are never judged here. Your authentic self knows all. It is whole, perfect and complete. It is total unconditional love and peace. Deepak Chopra defines the true self as "the field of possibilities, creativity, intentions, and power."[19] When you connect with this Source Energy of your authentic self, all is well in you and the world no matter how it looks on the outside.

It is the objective of the LAM Mindfulness Curriculum to guide both parents and professionals home to their authentic or true selves. ***This is the place where you will find the peace and the inner knowing that will empower you to help the child with special needs in the best possible way.*** The LAM Mindfulness Curriculum offers you the strategies to enter into this sacred space of truth within yourself.

As Tim Shriver states in his book, *Fully Alive*, "the breakthrough lesson is that all life is beautiful… the most marginalized people in the world were well-acquainted with suffering but also masters of healing. They taught me that we are all totally vulnerable and totally valuable at the same time… the athletes of Special Olympics taught me more about how to see than what to see…there's another way of seeing: from the inside out."[20] The LAM Mindfulness Curriculum offers you the strategies to move from the outside ego to the inside authentic self.

HOW DOES ONE MOVE FROM THE EGO TO THE AUTHENTIC SELF?

Moving from the ego to the authentic self is not an easy task. It is absolutely necessary to do if you want to experience harmony, peace and joy in your life while achieving the best possible outcome for the child. How do you accomplish this?

First, you have to choose to have the willingness to make a change in your perception of life and of the child's potential. For example, if you view the world as the glass being "half empty", then you are in your "ego" and are more prone to perceive the child with special needs as "defective" or "damaged" goods. You are looking at the child from an outer perspective that is based on the physical world's perception of success.

In Tim Shriver's book, *Fully Alive*, he talks about the countless negative labels that have been given to people with special needs. He states, "…they each would have heard "retard", "defective", "sick", "delayed" and maybe worst of all, "in-valid." Success experiences were nonexistent. Gentleness in the company of strangers was rare. Acceptance among peers was a distant dream. 'I am never', one parent of a child with special needs wept, 'able to be proud of my child'."[21] As you can see, this labeling only creates a negative environment for you and the child believing that the child needs "fixing" instead of "coaching" and "support". You begin to believe that the child has limitations instead of limitless possibilities. With this mindset, you create artificial barriers to the child's success and development. If you as the parent or professional limit the child's potential, then how in the world can the child believe in himself/herself? It is LAM's opinion that if this limited perception persists as the overriding belief for the child, then all the therapy in the world will not allow for the full expression of the child's development and gifts.

Now, let's see how changing your perception from the glass being "half empty" to "half full" changes the way you view the child and his or her potential. When your perception of the glass is "half full," you start to live from your authentic self instead of from your ego. Living in your authentic self allows you to be in touch with your inner knowing. You feel a sense of peace and calmness and are less reactive. As a parent, you trust yourself as the "Captain" of your own ship as well as that of the child's ship. As a professional, you start to use your intuition as well as your expertise to guide the child. Fear, shame, unworthiness and guilt cannot co-exist in your authentic self. As previously mentioned, your authentic self is perfect, whole and complete. It does not judge oneself or others. You start to view the child's essence as perfect and whole. You don't experience pain from the past or anxiety about the future. You exist in the present moment to do your best for the child. Limitless possibilities for the child exist in your authentic self. As a parent, you lovingly guide the professionals who will help your child based on your inner knowing. As a professional, you realize the importance of the parent's support in the therapeutic process and listen to the parent's wisdom. Both as parents and professionals, you are choosing to live from the core of your being which is unconditional love for yourself and the child. This environment creates the safe space at the "LAM Buffet." Now, the parent, child and professional will flourish and move forward on the path to "changing the system."

HOW DOES THE LAM MINDFULNESS CURRICULUM OFFER YOU THE STRATEGIES TO MOVE YOU FROM THE EGO TO THE AUTHENTIC SELF?

Before you as parents and professionals attend the LAM Buffet, let's take a little side trip and learn the strategies that will help you move from your ego to authentic self. Now that you are familiar with the definitions of both the ego and the authentic self, you are ready to learn the strategies that will allow you to live from your authentic self. We say at LAM that this is living from the inside out. In other words, your inner world dictates your outer expression in the physical world. You don't have to relinquish anything here. Both your ego and authentic self can co-exist. Each plays an important role in your life. Your authentic self is now the "driver" instead of the "passenger." The "ego" becomes the "passenger" instead of the "driver." The captain of your ship, therefore, is your true or authentic self. The ego is along for the ride. How will you know when this has occurred? You will experience more peace and become a "witness" or "observer" of yourself and of the child. In addition, you will become less reactive and more proactive in a loving manner.

According to Deepak Chopra, "We can go beyond the ego through self awareness - awareness of our thoughts, feelings, behaviors, and speech." [22] Our LAM Mindfulness Curriculum offers you the strategies that will take you to this new level of self-awareness.

The LAM MINDFULNESS CURRICULUM STRATEGIES

Learning the LAM Mindfulness Curriculum strategies helps you to create the safe space which is the foundation or "table" of the "LAM Buffet."

BREATHWORK

Notice your Breath

Breathwork is conscious breathing. Find a quiet space where you will not be interrupted for at least five minutes. While standing, sitting or lying on your back, close your eyes and just notice the inflow and outflow of your breath. Begin to watch your breath like the waves of the ocean. Begin to count how long it takes to inhale and exhale. Begin to notice the origins of your breath. Are you breathing from your shoulders and head? Or are you breathing from your chest? Or are you breathing from your lower abdomen? Are you nose breathing? Are you mouth breathing? Just notice where the breath is coming from and feel that breath. There is no judgment here. This is the beginning of breathing mindfully. The object of any conscious breathwork is to stay focused in the present moment with your breath.

Square Breathing

Another simple exercise can be done while standing, sitting or lying on your back. Inhale through the nose to the count of four and exhale through the nose to the count of four. If this is too difficult for you, reduce the count on both the inhalation and the exhalation. If the nose is stuffed, breathe through the mouth. The purpose of the exercise is to relax you and not strain you. "All breathing practices should be done without strain or building up pressure." [23]

Stress Relieving Breath

This exercise can be done while standing, sitting, or lying on your back. It's similar to Square Breathing but the exhalation is longer than the inhalation. Inhale through the nose to the count of four and exhale through the nose to the count of five or six. If this causes strain or build-up of pressure, reduce the counts or breathe through the mouth. Do this exercise three times. Return to your normal breath and notice how much calmer you feel. If three times is not enough to calm you, then repeat the exercise again for three more times and return to your normal breath.

Three Part Breath or Complete Breath

This breathing exercise should be done lying down on your back. Inhale through the nose in three parts. First, fill your lower abdomen with breath, then the rib cage and lastly the upper chest. Exhale the breath fully. Do this exercise slowly three times and then let your breath return to normal. Once your breathing is back to normal for a minute or so, you can reverse this exercise as follows. Inhale fully to the upper chest. Next, exhale a little sip of breath from the upper chest, then into your middle ribs and then into your lower abdomen. Exhale fully and completely to release the breath. Do this exercise slowly three times and then let your breath completely return to normal.

Complex Breathing Practices

If you are interested in learning more complex breathing practices such as Alternate Nostril Breathing, Kapalabhati breathing, Breath of Fire, Ujjayi, Sitali, and Sitkari breathing practices, please consult your local registered yoga teacher for hands-on guidance. Do not attempt any breath retention or any complicated breathing practice without proper training. When complex breathing practices are done improperly, they can be harmful to both your mental and physical health.

In conclusion, breathing mindfully quiets the ego and allows you to discover an awareness of your authentic self. Your authentic self has been there all along but now you are uncovering it mindfully and allowing it to emerge. Breathing practices require patience, persistence and consistency in order to reap rewards. Once you have achieved a level of mindfulness and awareness of your authentic self, you can return "home" to this safe space at any time. This is your sacred space. You have come home to your true self.

QIGONG

Qigong is an ancient Chinese self-healing practice that seeks to promote balance in the body, mind and spirit. Roger Jahnke's book, *The Healer Within,* says, "Your body, in cooperation with your mind and spirit, is marvelously blessed with miraculous self-healing abilities."[24]

Qigong involves the use of the "Four Baskets of Practice" that are the following: movement and body-oriented practices, breath-oriented practices (similar to yoga breathing practices), meditation (similar to yoga), and self-applied massage. In order to practice Qigong, it is recommended to find a licensed practitioner in your area.

We at LAM attended one of Roger Jahnke's Qigong workshops offered by The Institute of Integral Qigong and Tai Chi. We have incorporated many of his practices into our LAM Mindfulness Curriculum workshops.

The value of practicing Qigong consistently will help both professionals and parents move from their egos into their authentic selves. Qigong creates grounding, centeredness, focus and peacefulness. This is invaluable when encountering any new and unfamiliar situation with the child. Through the creation of a safe space, the child will feel love and acceptance. This is especially important for professionals who work with children with special needs. A safe therapeutic space allows the professional and the child to meet stated goals and objectives effortlessly. By practicing Qigong, the professional may become more relaxed and less likely to experience professional burnout. In addition, the parent becomes more relaxed and less reactive to negative behavioral situations.

YOGA MOVEMENT AND OTHER RESTORATIVE PRACTICES

The purpose of yoga movement and other restorative movement practices is to promote balance. Yoga means "union" of body, mind and spirit. With yoga movement, one learns how to stay fully present and focused in the body while practicing certain poses or "asanas." The physical movement accompanied by breathwork allows the body to ground, expand, and release any emotion, stress, or tension in muscles, fascia or bodily tissues. By calming the mind and the physical body, neuro-chemicals are released that allow the mind and body to be in the parasympathetic mode that is the body's relaxation or healing state. The spirit or authentic self now has a chance to emerge once the body and mind are clear.

Restorative practices specifically try to open or release tension in the physical and emotional body while promoting balance and healing wherever needed. This involves the use of "props" or "supports" such as bolsters, blocks or blankets. The use of these "props" facilitates greater relaxation and releasing of any chronic tension, stress or strong emotions in the body. It is not unusual for various negative emotions to surface and release during restorative movement practices.

We at LAM have used the techniques of both yoga movement and restorative practices in our past Mindfulness Curriculum workshops. These practices are also offered all over the country at yoga studios. We have observed that both yoga and restorative practices are invaluable for releasing stress or tension in both parents of children with special needs and the professionals who work with them. Parents who have experienced these practices in our LAM Mindfulness Curriculum Workshops often described it as "going to a spa", "taking time for myself" and "opening up to seeing my child in a more loving and supportive way". Yoga movement and other restorative practices are excellent strategies to move you from your ego to your authentic self.

MEDITATION

Breathwork, Qigong, yoga movement and restorative movement practice are all different strategies that prepare you for experiencing meditation. Louise Hay, a famous metaphysical healer and teacher, states, "meditation is when we sit down and turn off our inner dialogue long enough to hear our own wisdom...sometimes, we think we're supposed to fix everything in our lives, and maybe we're really only supposed to learn something from the situation."[25]

LAM believes that meditation is a process in which one quiets the ego mind of all thoughts and physical distractions so that the authentic self can truly emerge. It is a practice of just "being" and not "doing." When meditating, you exist in the present moment. This means that you do not regret or suffer past experiences or worry about the future. Meditation is especially important for parents of children with special needs who suffer from tremendous shame or guilt that in some way they are responsible for their child's challenges. Parents may also worry about the future of their child with special needs becoming an independent adult. Meditation changes the parent's paradigm from "fixing" to "supporting" his/her child in a positive manner. For professionals, meditation quiets the ego mind and allows the authentic self to emerge and to be the dominant force during the therapeutic process.

As a result of meditation, the parent/professional's belief shifts from "fixing" to "supporting" the child with special needs. This new LAM paradigm releases parents from past regrets, shame or guilt. The future is now viewed as something that they will co-create with their child filled with limitless possibilities instead of worry. For professionals, the emphasis shifts to the present moment. Instead of viewing the child from past achievements or future goals, the role of the professional becomes one of support and guidance with no limitations based only on checklists.

Meditation has its origins in all wisdom traditions that have been in practice for thousands of years. All religious traditions practice some form of meditation or prayer. This versatile practice can be executed while sitting, lying down or standing. There is no right way to meditate. We can offer you now the following types of meditation practices to help you move from your ego to your authentic self: moving meditation, guided meditation, visualization, mantra meditations with the use of hand gestures called "mudras" and affirmations.

Moving meditation

Mindful walking with and without eyes closed being aware of every step and every person in the room.

Guided meditation

This type of meditation is usually done in some restorative yoga pose or lying down on the floor. The student is guided in exploring different feelings or internal states in the body. Focus varies depending on what the participant needs at that particular time. Some examples are grounding meditations, heart-centered meditations, and healing meditations.

Visualization

Visualization is very similar to a guided meditation but allows you to choose specific images that conjure up feelings of love, joy, peace, grounding, safety and/or nurturing. You are guided to create your own internal canvas of solitude and can return to this safe space at any time you choose. For example, imagine yourself on a beach. What is the weather like? What does the beach feel like? How big are the waves? What are the colors you see? What is the temperature you feel? What does the wind against your skin feel like? How warm is the sand and so on...

The purpose of visualization is to allow you to visit your safe space anytime you need. This safe space empowers you to deal with any external challenges or stressors you may experience in a positive way. Your paradigm shifts from feeling as if you are a victim of your circumstances to feeling as if you are a conscious co-creator of your own life.

Mantras/Mudras Used During Meditation

Mantras are words or phrases repeated over and over again silently to yourself while you sit quietly practicing meditation. Mantras provide the ego mind with something to do so that the distracting thoughts don't overwhelm the authentic self. Mudras are hand gestures that have an effect on the energy flow of the body. Two examples of frequently used mudras by LAM are the following:

1. Positioning of the hands at the heart center in a prayer position.
2. Positioning of the hands on the thighs with the palms facing up while joining the thumb with each finger of any hand. The positioning of the thumb with each of the fingers facilitates a particular flow of energy for that position. Each finger represents a particular quality that can be enhanced when positioned with the thumb. The forefinger represents wisdom. The middle finger represents patience. The ring finger

represents creativity or intuition. The pinky finger represents open and honest communication.

When used together, mantras and mudras provide the means for you to concentrate in the present moment without any physical or external distraction while creating a positive energy flow in the body, mind and spirit.

Affirmations

Louise Hay, one of the most famous metaphysical healers and teachers of our time has used the full potential of affirmations in her writings and lectures to create personal growth and self-healing in many thousands of people over the last fifty years. An affirmation is a positive statement that is said over and over again to oneself to re-wire the brain into thinking that the glass is half-full instead of half-empty.

Affirmations re-program both the conscious and unconscious mind into a new more positive way of thinking that promotes healing and balance in the mind, body, and spirit. Some examples are:

> All is well in me.
> I can do it.
> I am perfect, whole and complete.
> My child is perfect, whole and complete.
> All that happens is in divine order.
> I radiate peace and serenity.
> My child is a gift.
> The future is filled with limitless possibilities.
> I am the present moment.
> I am who I am.
> Let go.

The possibilities are endless! You can create your own. Louise Hay suggests saying these affirmations everyday often while looking in the mirror.[26]

HANDS-ON LAM ENERGY WORK:

As mentioned in Chapter Two, LAM Energy work is the "glue" or cornerstone of our LAM Mindfulness Curriculum. It teaches the parent/professional how to use "intention" to move energy for the highest possible good in themselves and in the child. In past LAM Mindfulness Training Workshops, the LAM practitioner practiced the LAM energy work on each participant individually. This facilitated the participant's ability to feel grounded and nurtured and allowed for the possibility of releasing negative emotions or belief patterns that may have been hindering that participant's ability to connect with his/her authentic self. This energy work consisted of channeling love, peace, grounding, and nurturing in order to create a safe space for each participant. LAM Energy work facilitated a meditative state. Parents and professionals were able to learn how to use these techniques first on themselves during challenging life situations. As the participants became more comfortable using these techniques, they were then able to practice using them on the child with special needs whenever needed. As the participants learned, it required consistent practice and patience to use LAM Energy work effectively.

JOURNALING:

Journaling is a very important component of the LAM Mindfulness Curriculum. We suggest journaling after meditation when you can contemplate from your authentic self and write down whatever comes to mind. It's completely up to you whether or not you wish to share your responses with anyone. The act of writing itself helps solidify and clarify any outstanding issues you may be facing.

OUTCOMES OF LAM MINDFULNESS TRAINING CURRICULUM

The first outcome of the LAM Mindfulness Curriculum is the movement from negative belief patterns to more positive ones in order to live in your authentic self. The negative belief patterns you possess limit your potential. They don't allow your true authentic self to be revealed. When you are living with negative belief patterns, you may feel that you are "missing" something. You may even be on a quest of "searching" for that "missing something." When you don't align with your true authentic self, you feel disconnected and isolated even in a group of people who support you. It's the "illusion" of what your life "should" be instead of what it truly is. These patterns make you feel sad, anxious, unworthy, depressed and unlovable. Examples include: "I am not good enough. I am unworthy. I am unlovable. I am imperfect. I need help all the time. I can't do it. I'm not strong enough. I am not capable. I lack resources. Life is a struggle." These patterns can create "dis-ease" even in the strongest among us. As human beings, we all have at least one or some of these patterns.

The second outcome is the elimination of limited cultural conditioning. This occurs when traditions are enacted over and over again. These traditions are handed down consciously and subconsciously as a set of rules and regulations. If you are to be an accepted member of the family tribe, you must follow these rules and regulations. They involve your religious traditions, education, and family beliefs about what is most important to be successful in life. Examples of cultural conditioning include:

To be a good person and fit into the family tribe, you must:
1. Go to your religious institution and follow all those rules;
2. Go to school and follow all of those rules;
3. Always listen to your parents or elders in the family under all conditions;
4. Make a good living;
5. Pursue higher education;
6. Have your own family with children.
7. Obey all professionals as "experts" such as law enforcement officers, doctors, lawyers, teachers, etc.

As you notice, these examples are ways in which we all navigate society. It becomes problematic when these examples do not align with your true authentic self and limit the fulfillment of your true potential. So, if you abide by this conditioning when your authentic or true self doesn't feel aligned with these principles, you experience angst. You reach a choice point of either living by the rules and sacrificing who you truly are or you decide to break from conditioned patterns. Either way, you will experience confusion and some positive and negative emotions. This is why the LAM Mindfulness Curriculum is so very important. It safely guides you home to your authentic self.

The third outcome of the LAM Mindfulness Curriculum is that it teaches you how to relax. You will learn how to put your body into the healing mode of the parasympathetic nervous system. All of the Mindfulness Curriculum strategies will facilitate this process. Physiological relaxation responses such as lowered blood pressure and heart rate will occur. Emotionally, you will feel very peaceful and calm. This outcome allows you to achieve the next outcome effortlessly.

The fourth outcome of the LAM Mindfulness Curriculum is the confidence to take a deep breath and observe the stressful events in your own life as a "witness" rather than as a "reactor." The child with special needs will benefit directly and indirectly from your own transformation first and foremost. A direct benefit of this ability to "witness" your life instead of "reacting" to it is that you will stay in the parasympathetic response long enough to remain calm and focused when dealing with the child's challenging behaviors. An indirect benefit of this phenomenon is that the child will pick up your calm and focused energy. Instead of becoming more frantic, the child will calm down and exhibit more appropriate behaviors.

Lastly, the final outcome of the LAM Mindfulness Curriculum is the creation of a greater sense of self-awareness, self-acceptance, and unconditional love for your authentic self. As your authentic self becomes the "captain" of your ship, you will experience a more expanded sense of yourself. Negative emotions will not rule your life in the same way anymore. You will feel greater self-love and self- acceptance. You will also feel freer, lighter and more confident in your own personal journey and with that of the child. Whether you are a parent or professional, life will flow more seamlessly and with less effort.

Accept it all. It is all part of the process of becoming whole and changing the paradigm between you and the child from "fixing" to "supporting." All will emerge from this chrysalis like butterflies. Congratulations! You have completed the LAM Mindfulness Curriculum training and are now invited to attend the LAM Buffet.

Chapter 4

Traditional Modalities Used In The LAM Program

Here at LAM, the use of traditional Western therapeutic modalities was essential to the LAM program. The primary purpose of these modalities as part of the "LAM Buffet" was to provide a "way in" to the child's world that is safe and familiar. These modalities facilitated the creation of the safe space for the child. It also allowed the child to feel comfortable in experiencing the unfamiliar non-traditional modalities. The LAM program is keenly aware that the professionals who are currently reading this book have received already the appropriate professional training in their particular discipline. The LAM program realizes this fact. Therefore, our forthcoming explanation will be directed specifically to the parents of children with special needs.

Each traditional therapeutic modality must be specific and tailored to the unique needs of the child. To determine which one would work best to achieve the best outcome, the LAM practitioner observed the child's responses to the various stimuli provided. For example, was the child engaged and attentive to the task presented? Did he or she resist the task? Did the child comply with the task or feel frustrated? If the child appeared to be at ease and comfortable with performing a particular task in a traditional modality, then the LAM practitioner could continue with that task. If not, then the task or modality would be switched until attention and compliance occurred. Positive reinforcement was used on an as needed basis to encourage compliance. At LAM, it was imperative to create a higher energetic vibration of love and acceptance with the child when performing these traditional tasks.

This built a bridge for the LAM practitioner to gain access to the child's inherent abilities and weaknesses. This bridge forged a bond of trust not only between the child and practitioner but also between the child and the parent.

Much has been written about traditional therapeutic modalities. It is not LAM's intention to describe each of these modalities in detail but rather to describe its particular role in the "LAM Buffet" and its efficacy where appropriate. LAM believed in using the following traditional therapeutic modalities to create the safe space or "LAM Buffet Table." They are Play therapy, Gross Motor therapy, Sensory activities, and Speech/Cognitive therapy. Let's examine each one in detail as it applied to the LAM program.

PLAY THERAPY

Playing with a child with special needs is critical to his or her development especially during the first three years of life. We at LAM believe that as a parent it is absolutely essential that you engage the child in some form of interactive play. This is not an easy task since the child is usually delayed or disconnected socially. Typically, you as the parent may feel frustrated and unrewarded from the lack of reciprocity when heartfelt smiles, coos, eye contact, and gestures are not exchanged. In other words, the child's lack of responsiveness creates an energetic block of sadness or defeat that stops you from continuing the communicative exchange. As a result, you disconnect from the child feeling sadness and despair when he or she needs you the most. At LAM, we understand that you as parents need a lot of love and support to cope with this extra burden of not being able to engage your child easily in play. But, you must not give up. Play is how children learn about the world, grow and develop. Many professionals can teach you how to play purposefully with your child. We at LAM can give you some pointers in the right direction.

PLAY DO'S AND DON'TS:

1. DO SHUT OFF ALL TECHNOLOGY. To be fully present with your child, you must refrain from using all technology during your playtime.

2. DON'T USE TECHNOLOGY SUCH AS IPADS, IPHONES, COMPUTERS TO CAPTIVATE YOUR CHILD'S ATTENTION. Many studies have shown how detrimental the use of "screen time" is to a child's growing brain. Studies have reported that increased usage of screen time actually reduced a child's attention and motivation to communicate verbally. In fact, "television and other entertainment media should be avoided for infants and children under age two. A child's brain develops rapidly during these first years, and young children learn best by interacting with people, not screens"[27].

3. DO OBSERVE YOUR CHILD WHEN YOUR CHILD IS IN A HAPPY AND CONTENTED PLACE. In other words, notice when, where and how your child reacts to his or her environment in a positive manner. Even for infants, there are moments of complete contentment and surrender. You will know when these moments occur. This is the most productive time to engage your child in some sort of play. Since your child feels safe and loved, you will have the best opportunity to connect with your child in a joyful and effortless way. Even if you notice only fleeting moments, seize them as opportunities to be fully present and engaged with your child in a playful way. You will both feel love and acceptance. Reciprocity will occur. The moments will become longer and longer since you both will enjoy a higher energetic vibration of being fully present together.

4. DON'T GET DISCOURAGED IF YOUR CHILD REFUSES TO PLAY YOUR GAME. Many times you will have to switch to a game that your child wants to play. This may require switching often until you find an activity that is mutually enjoyable to both of you. Do this in a playful and non-judgmental manner. Do not exhibit frustration, annoyance or judgment if your child doesn't want to comply. As the parent, you still are in charge but please do not try to control or dictate the type of activity all the time. At every opportunity, the child needs to

have controlled choices in order to feel supported, loved and accepted. So, ease up a bit on the need to control every aspect of your child's life. The trick here is to balance your child-like and adult nature so that you can meet your child on his or her level while still maintaining a safe structure for the play in which to occur. Playing creates the highest energetic vibrations of joy and love. Have fun here! Remember to smile and enjoy yourself.

5. DO ENCOURAGE THE USE OF THESE TYPES OF MANIPULATIVE AND PRETEND PLAY ACTIVITIES.
   a) Blocks, legos, peg boards, pop-up toys, ring stackers
   b) Large picture books and books of any variety with textures and tabs
   c) Puzzles
   d) Puppets/dolls
   e) Pretend kitchen activities of cooking, eating and drinking
   f) Pretend household tasks of cleaning, vacuuming, etc.
   g) Pretend personal hygiene care
   h) Pretend doctor/nurse
   i) Pretend dollhouse, farm, school and transportation
   j) Pretend dress-up
   k) Musical instruments
   l) Sticker books

6. DON'T USE TOYS THAT SPEAK OR HAVE LIGHTS OR SOUND. Avoid toys that are technology-based or leave little room for the child to interact in an imaginative manner. These toys are over-stimulating just like any other piece of technology and could be harmful to brain development. They do not create the safe space or the "LAM Buffet Table" that is desired when playing with your child.

CASE STUDY NUMBER 8:
GEORGE G. AND STEVEN

George, a seven-year-old boy, was diagnosed with moderate autism, sensory processing disorder and a disturbance in gross motor skills as evidenced by toe walking, low muscle tone and difficulty skipping. He received Occupational, Physical and Speech Therapies in addition to Applied Behavioral Analysis Therapy in a self-contained special education school. His father Steven accompanied George to most of the LAM therapy sessions.

When George initially came to see us, he was verbal but unable to express fully his wants and needs consistently. He exhibited perseveration, self-stimulating behaviors of facial twitching and toe walking. We saw George for approximately ten sessions over the course of six months. During the first seven sessions, he improved dramatically in the areas of expressive language, empathy and age-appropriate behaviors. At the third session, after trial and error with the other modalities at the "LAM Buffet," the LAM practitioners discovered happily that stuffed animals and puppets were George's activity of choice. From that point on, the LAM practitioners used pretend play activities to create and maintain the safe space for George.

He gradually began to express spontaneously how the toys felt. He would say, "He needs support and his heart hurts." While saying this, George would wrap an ace bandage around the stuffed animal's face, mouth and heart. While this pretend play was occurring, the LAM practitioners were doing LAM Energy work to maintain the safe space. During the fourth session of pretend play, the dialogue changed spontaneously. Now, George was saying, "I am sad. My heart hurts. I'm gonna fix my heart." This dialogue all occurred while George bandaged the stuffed animal and the LAM practitioners continued the LAM Energy work. At the sixth session, a toy doctor's kit was introduced and another transformational shift occurred. Now, George used the doctor's kit on himself and on the stuffed animal to make himself and the stuffed animal feel better. An even more dramatic transformational release occurred during the seventh session. This time George was able to state his own feelings of sadness. He told the LAM practitioners that the bandages he applied to himself would make him feel better. At the eighth session, Steven, George's Dad, reported "significant spontaneous language at home." George was reported to initiate and maintain a conversation of about three turns on a topic that was contextually relevant to both the speaker and the listener. In other words, George was now exhibiting age-appropriate social language skills. The LAM practitioners and George's dad were thrilled!

Unfortunately, during the last three sessions, the LAM practitioners observed a regression in George's hard-earned skills. This regression was attributed to the large gap in time between sessions of two unstructured summer months. The parents decided to discontinue the LAM sessions due to personal concerns.

Finding the traditional modality of play helped George feel safe. Once the safe space was attained, the LAM Energy work became the critical bridge that enabled George to achieve developmental milestones that were formerly unattainable. We also concluded that parents of children with special needs must understand how very important it is to engage in any form of play with their child even though they may not receive an abundance of "feedback."

In conclusion, play creates an energetic transfer of love and acceptance when done without judgment or preconceived outcomes. Due to the lack of spontaneous feedback, it may not seem like play to you. Try to be patient, compassionate, and fun loving when engaging in play with your child. Your child must feel safe, supported, nurtured and loved. This is the very reason why LAM recommends the LAM Mindfulness Curriculum for parents. See prior Chapter 3 for complete details.

GROSS MOTOR THERAPY

Gross motor therapy targets gross motor skills. Gross motor skills "involve the large muscles of the body that enable such functions as walking, kicking, sitting upright, lifting, and throwing a ball."[28] LAM used gross motor skills commonly called "exercise" to engage the child and the parent in fun movements and activities that promote the development of large muscles and cardiovascular health. "While most of us focus on exercise as a way to trim our waistlines, the better news is that routine physical activity firms up the brain—making it a simple, alternative ADHD treatment."[29] Gross motor skills are essential for grounding and releasing frenetic energy or stress. During gross motor activities, the parasympathetic nervous system gets activated while the sympathetic nervous system gets de-activated. Everyone starts to relax and feel good.

GROSS MOTOR ACTIVITIES

1. Exercise balls for rolling and sitting
2. Scooter games to ground and improve core stability
3. Running, dancing, jumping and hopping to music using spots on floor and large silks
4. "Freeze" games with music and movements
5. Use of parachute with bean bags
6. Rolling and catching balls
7. Tunnel play
8. Imitation of whole body movement games (e.g. "Follow the Leader")

Note: Have fun and do these activities in a joyful and playful manner with the child. Remember to balance your child-like and adult-like nature to create the optimal safe space. If the child is still displaying hyperactivity and impulsivity, it is imperative to repeat the gross motor activities that keep the child close to the floor such as rolling, tunnel play and scooters on stomach. These activities will allow the energy of the child to move downward into the ground ("grounding exercise").

SENSORY ACTIVITIES

As LAM practitioners, we incorporated some of these sensory activities into our program since many or most of the children we saw had displayed one or more symptoms of Sensory Integration or Sensory Processing Disorder. We chose these activities because we wanted the child to feel safe, secure and grounded. In other words, we attempted to create the safe space necessary for the LAM Buffet. Parents should not try to do any of these sensory activities without the guidance of a professional Occupational Therapist. Parents and caregivers are not able to deal with these issues alone. We at LAM often referred our children to Occupational Therapy first before they entered into our program. If the underlying Sensory Processing Disorder was too great, then we usually eliminated the "trigger" or "triggers" that would have caused the overload in the child when they were participating in the LAM program. It was not necessary for us at LAM to have provided that sensory experience if it created too much distress for the child. Our goal was NOT to de-sensitize the child to the sensory experiences per se but rather to create the safe space.

"*Sensory Processing* (sometimes called 'sensory integration' or SI) is a term that refers to the way the nervous system receives messages from the senses and turns them into appropriate motor and behavioral responses. *Sensory Processing Disorder* (SPD, formerly known as 'sensory integration dysfunction') is a condition that exists when sensory signals *don't* get organized into appropriate responses. Pioneering occupational therapist and neuroscientist, A. Jean Ayres, PhD, likened Sensory Processing Disorder to a neurological 'traffic jam' that prevents certain parts of the brain from receiving the information needed to interpret sensory information correctly. A person with Sensory Processing Disorder finds it difficult to process and act upon information received through the senses, which creates challenges in performing countless everyday tasks. Motor clumsiness, behavioral problems, anxiety, depression, school failure, and other impacts may result if the disorder is not treated effectively."[30]

At LAM, depending on the child's particular Sensory Processing Disorder, we determined which sensory activities were best for creating the optimal safe space for that particular child and what the occupational therapist had recommended as a "sensory diet." "A 'sensory diet' (coined by occupational therapist Patricia Wilbarger) is a carefully designed personalized activity plan that provides the sensory input a person needs to stay focused and organized throughout the day... Each child has a unique set of sensory needs. Generally, a child whose nervous system is on 'high trigger or too wired' needs more calming input, while the child who is more 'sluggish or too tired' needs more arousing input. A qualified OT can use his/her advanced training and evaluation skills to develop a good sensory diet for your child." [31]

At LAM, this "sensory diet" allowed the child to feel calm and peaceful which facilitated the creation of the LAM safe space. That was our principal goal. Without the creation of the safe space, there could be no LAM Buffet.

As a parent or caregiver, we know you are well aware of your child's sensory issues and their triggers. We at LAM had to determine the type of sensory issues that were present in a particular child first before choosing to engage in any sensory activity. How did the LAM practitioner choose? We at LAM believed it was very important to obtain a thorough case history from the parent before we even saw the child for the first time. This included a detailed discussion of the type or types of sensory issues that may have been underlying the child's difficult behaviors such as meltdowns, tantrums, separation anxiety, hiding, head banging, head holding, etc. LAM believed that each parent knew the "triggers" for these behaviors and how to avoid them. Once we recognized these "triggers," we came up with a specific plan to create the safest space for the child in a playful and trusting environment. We used or avoided a particular sensory activity while observing the child's reactions cautiously every step of the way. If the child displayed any emotional or physical discomfort or resistance, we had to change the activity and try again later. Eventually, we broke through the discomfort. It was a very slow process. It involved a lot of patience, understanding, love and trust.

Please note that if at any time a parent or practitioner's frustration is apparent to the child, then the energetic bond of trust will be broken and the sensory activity should be discontinued immediately. That is the very reason why we recommend referrals to traditional occupational therapists for Sensory Processing Disorder. *Without any formal training* from occupational therapists, parents should not try to use sensory activities on their own. It may be more detrimental than helpful.

TYPES OF SENSORY ACTIVITIES

1) Tunnel:

The child would crawl through a tunnel, throw a ball into it, or roll in it. A child who enjoyed playing with a tunnel benefited from its grounding and centering properties.

2) Floor exercises in blankets/mats:

Floor exercises such as rolling in blankets or mats provided sensory stimulation for grounding and centering.

3) Deep Pressure/Massage:

If the child could tolerate or enjoy touch to the upper and lower extremities, deep pressure and/or gentle massage would be used to relax the muscles and stimulate the response of the parasympathetic nervous system.

4) Sound therapy (music/bowls/instruments):

Sound therapy was used only for those children who enjoyed and tolerated auditory stimulation. LAM noticed that some hypersensitive children would have difficulty tolerating different degrees of auditory stimulation and that this might create discomfort. Therefore, sound therapy was used on an individualized basis. It is important to note that the benefits of sound therapy as a healing tool have been well documented.

5) Tactile input (silk scarves, cotton balls, different-textured fabrics):

Tactile input through the use of silk scarves, cotton balls and different textured fabrics was used for those children who craved tactile input and enjoyed feeling something against their skin.

6) Walking or hopping onto plastic discs on floor/hula hoops:

Walking or hopping onto plastic discs that were of different shapes and colors were used to provide visual and tactile stimulation. Hula Hoops were sometimes used to denote a child's sense of personal space by creating a concrete boundary. We noticed that many children with sensory issues either had no sense of boundaries altogether or were too rigid in protecting their own boundaries. We found this activity to be very helpful for most of the children who participated in our LAM Program.

7) Parachutes:

Parachutes were used in a number of ways in our LAM program. First, we had the child hold an edge of the parachute and work as a team to raise and lower it. Second, we had the child sit on the parachute and the LAM practitioners and parent would spin the child. Third, we threw balls or beanbags into it with the objective of the activity to keep the ball or beanbag elevated in the parachute. Fourth, we had the child run under the raised parachute or lie down under it. The option of raising or lowering the parachute would be left up to that particular child if he/she were capable of making that decision.

8) Exercise Balls:

Rolling on exercise balls were used to create proprioception or an awareness of the body in space. It created a kinesthetic awareness of the core muscles in the body.

In conclusion, these are just a few of the examples of the types of sensory activities that were used in the LAM program. The ultimate aim of each of these activities was to create the desired outcome of well being in the child. *Remember, first and foremost, these activities were used by the LAM practitioners to create a safe space.*

SPEECH/COGNITIVE THERAPY:

Adrienne Murphy, one of the co-creators of the LAM program, is a veteran speech-language pathologist. We had incorporated this modality extensively in our LAM program. Many children we saw lacked the necessary skills to express their wants or needs consistently and exhibited compensatory negative behaviors such as hitting, crying, biting, etc. when expressive communication skills were impaired or delayed. Some children did not even have the pre-requisite communication skills when they entered into our LAM program. These lacking pre-requisite skills were: eye contact, joint attention, turn-taking skills, attention or focus, pointing and vocalizing. Here at LAM, we met the child at his or her own particular communication level and created a playful environment that stimulated the child's motivation to engage with the LAM practitioners and the parent/caregiver. If the child exhibited frustration at any time, the LAM practitioner would change the task or attempt the same task with the use of some form of token positive reinforcement. *The primary goal of any communicative exchange with the child was to create the safe space and the high energetic vibrations of love and acceptance.*

TYPES OF SPEECH ACTIVITIES

1. Repetition Drills: The LAM practitioner used simple sounds or words/word approximations to encourage the child to communicate verbally at the optimum level. Example: The LAM practitioner held up a ball to the non/pre-verbal child and required that the child respond with some sound or approximation of "ball" before allowing the child to play with the ball.

2. Physical/Tactile/Gestural/Visual Prompts: These are different types of cues used by a speech therapist to facilitate speech sound development or vocal expression. Physical prompts would be used around the child's mouth to create the shape necessary for the vocalization of the sound/word. Tactile prompts were used on the oral musculature to help the child feel the spot where the sound originated. Gestural prompts are cues that were used to create an understanding of a particular word without the word being said, e.g. signing or waving bye. Visual prompts such as pictures/objects were used to heighten learning of the actual word being said (e.g. showing the child a ball while saying the word "ball"). It is important to realize that any parent or caregiver can learn how to use these prompts when shown by a speech pathologist.

3. Modeling: Acting out the action of a word or sentence (e.g. pushing a train while saying "choo choo"or blowing bubbles and saying "pop").

4. Role Playing: Form of pretend play that could involve the use of miniature figures or the representation of frequently used objects in everyday life (e. g. Little People walking up the stairs of a house, cooking with pots/pans, vacuuming with a toy vacuum, etc.). The child either used gestures or objects themselves to represent role-playing or actual words to create or describe the activity.

5. Asking/Answering Yes/No and Wh- (What, Where, Who, When, and Why) Questions: The LAM practitioner attempted to use these questions if the child's comprehension was at the age-appropriate level of understanding. Yes/no questions were used for the child with a lower level of comprehension. Wh- questions were used for the more advanced child since they required a more open-ended response. Typically, yes/no questions were used initially in a session. In later sessions, more advanced Wh- questions would be used as the child's language skills progressed.

6. Following Of Directions: This was used to increase a child's level of understanding or receptive language. It was customary for the LAM practitioner to start with the following of 1-step directions then progress to the following of 2-step directions and then to the following of multi-step directions. This was usually done during any play activity.

7. Creating Communicative Intent: This is the motivation to communicate. The first level of motivation for a young child is for requesting wants and needs. This was the most important speech activity used by the LAM practitioners since this not only created the safe space needed for the LAM Buffet but also helped the child to develop appropriate language skills.

In conclusion, traditional modalities were an integral part of our LAM program. The most important thing to remember is that their use can be extremely effective in creating the safe space at any time. However, each child is unique and different traditional modality usage requires a process of trial and error. It is LAM's belief that traditional modalities are extremely useful in the creation of the necessary safe space at the "LAM Buffet." It is important to remember to be loving, supportive and flexible. Children typically express how they feel in the moment. You will know when you have created the safe space for them to feel love and acceptance.

Although these traditional modalities were extremely important and effective in the creation of the safe space or "LAM table," their efficacy was even more potent when used with non-traditional modalities. The best-case scenario is to pick one traditional and one non-traditional modality to create the safe space. So, let's move forward and take a look at all the non-traditional therapy modalities used in the LAM program.

Chapter 5

Non-Traditional Modalities Used in the LAM Program with Parent/Professional/Child

The LAM program defines non-traditional modalities as those modalities that are holistic and have Eastern philosophical roots. They are not mainstream Western approaches. Examples of the LAM non-traditional modalities are:

- Yoga Movement/Asana Practice
- Breathing Instruction and Conscious Breathwork
- Qigong
- Mindfulness Training including age-appropriate Mantras/Affirmations/Mudras
- Meditation Strategies – Walking, Heart-Centered, Grounding, and Guided Visualization
- Sound Therapy/Music Therapy

As you can see, these modalities are some of the practices already discussed in Chapter Three : The LAM Mindfulness Curriculum (Parent/Professional Training). Now, we will explore these practices as applicable to the pediatric population. Although play therapy is considered a "traditional therapy" modality, the LAM program used play in conjunction with the use of these non-traditional modalities as well. Just as with the traditional modalities, every non-traditional modality was adapted to the child's unique level of development. There is no "one size fits all" approach here at LAM. If the child exhibited resistance or non-compliance with the use of any particular non-traditional modality, the LAM practitioner would attempt to use another one in a playful manner. First and foremost, the safe space had to be created and maintained while using any of these non-traditional therapy modalities. The safe space allows for the presence of trust between parent/child or professional/child. It is intangible but we all know when we are in a safe space. We feel peaceful and at ease in a safe space. We smile and are more willing to relax and engage.

Since children with special needs exhibit disturbances in their play skills that manifest as a lack of joint attention, the presence of perseveration, obsessive-compulsiveness, rigidity, low frustration tolerance and self-stimulation, the creation of the safe space is absolutely critical to their development. They live in a "war zone" ready for "battle" at any moment not quite sure where the battle is, who they can trust or how they can survive. We at LAM believe that these children are lacking the "software" in the brain necessary to engage in the physical world without fear and anxiety. They often display sensory disturbances that exacerbate the sympathetic nervous system's response in a "typical" play situation. For example, certain lights, sounds, smells, textures and tastes can trigger an exaggerated response in any child with sensory issues. Most of the children with special needs that we have encountered in our LAM program have one or more sensory issues and live in a "fight or flight" mode.

Just like their children, parents of children with special needs also live in a "fight or flight" mode or "war zone" since they are always ready for the worst behaviors or meltdowns to occur. Often, these parents feel like it's their fault when their children exhibit these meltdowns or anti-social behaviors. It's not unusual for them to feel embarrassment, shame, anxiety, depression and/or guilt. This is the very reason why LAM Non-Traditional Modalities are so effective in creating the safe space for successful connection and engagement between parent and child.

By adding the use of non-traditional modalities, the professional also has the option of creating the safe space more quickly in one's own therapeutic practice. So, whether you are a parent or a professional, the usefulness of the non-traditional modalities used in the LAM program cannot be underestimated. Let's examine these non-traditional modalities in greater detail.

YOGA MOVEMENT/ASANA PRACTICE

If the parent or professional is familiar with simple yoga movements, this is a very helpful tool. "Yoga works by engaging the whole body and mind, providing activities that incorporate learning styles such as visual, kinesthetic, musical, intuitive, and naturalist (the awareness of one's personal environment and interaction with nature). By providing students with inner resources- such as calming, centering, and self-acceptance- yoga helps them feel connected and whole."[32]

The philosophy of yoga is to join or "yoke" the body, mind and spirit. Here at LAM, we believe that children with special needs are especially susceptible to feeling disconnected or dissociated from their bodies. These children tend to exhibit sensory processing issues and/or behavioral issues. The energy they exhibit is usually hyperactive or hypoactive. If the energy is hyperactive, energy scanning by the LAM practitioner will reveal that the energy is rising out of the head. This hyperactive energy causes a disconnection from the body and is manifested by anxiety, inattention and/or impulsivity. If the child has hypoactive energy, LAM believes that there is a blockage of the energy flow in the brain. The brain is short-circuiting and shutting down. Nothing is moving. This disconnection between the head and the body manifests as inattention, lethargy, inactivity, depression and/or withdrawal.

To understand this more fully, think of a time when you were extremely anxious and over-stimulated. Think about how you felt in your body at that time. Were you too anxious to sit down? Were you pacing? Were you able to perform a complicated task such as driving without harming yourself or others? Did you fall? Were you dizzy? This is an example of hyperactive energy. Now, think of a time when you were overwhelmed by a traumatic experience such as an accident, death of a loved one, or overall devastating news. How did you feel? Did your breathing become shallow, incomplete or non-existent? Did you sigh uncontrollably? Did you feel as if you were paralyzed? Were you able to attend to the task at hand? Were you able to move or speak? This is an example of hypoactive energy flow.

LAM practitioners describe both of these experiences as being "out of body." In either case, yoga movement joins the body, mind and spirit by allowing the energy to flow in a balanced manner throughout the whole system. Yoga does this by activating the parasympathetic nervous system and de-activating the sympathetic nervous system. "The parasympathetic nervous system (PNS) and sympathetic nervous system (SNS) work together to help you cope with and respond to daily life…daily life brings a myriad of stresses that activate the sympathetic nervous system (SNS). Loud noises, flashing lights… activate the sympathetic, or 'fight or flight' mechanisms in your body. Neuropsychologist and meditation teacher Rick Hanson says, 'the PNS and the SNS are connected like a seesaw; when one goes up the other goes down.' A yoga practice encourages you to pay attention to the sensations in your body and your reactions to those sensations. People who practice yoga thus learn to be aware of and respond differently to stress-inducing thoughts and experiences so that the baseline of PNS (Parasympathetic Nervous System) can be maintained."[33]

For children with sensory processing issues, yoga balances the body and creates homeostasis. This is especially effective and an extremely valuable modality to choose at the "LAM Buffet." Yoga reconnects the brain or mind to the body. It calms, grounds and centers children with special needs. We strongly encourage anyone, especially parents of children with special needs, to explore local yoga classes at your local YMCA or various yoga studios. In LAM Mindfulness Curriculum workshops, we taught our clients how to do various restorative and simple asana practices for themselves and with the children. Since we at LAM believe that direct hands-on modeling, cueing and teaching are necessary for executing various yoga poses in a safe manner without injury, we urge you to find a licensed yoga teacher to help you explore yoga more fully.

Yoga for the Special Child/ A Therapeutic Approach for Infants and Children with Down Syndrome, Cerebral Palsy and Learning

Disabilities written by Sonia Sumar is a wonderful guide for using yoga with children with special needs. In her book, she describes in detail the techniques used at each developmental level. The impetus behind Ms. Sumar's exploration with yoga as a therapy technique for children with special needs was her own daughter, Roberta, who was born in 1972 with Down syndrome. In the initial part of her book, she describes experimenting with yoga as a new healing modality in order to move her daughter forward developmentally. At that time, she said, "I then began to practice yoga not just for myself, but primarily for Roberta, searching for a key that would unlock the door to a condition considered incurable by medical science."[34]

For children from birth to 6 months, Ms. Sumar describes, "…It is important for the yoga teacher to develop strong, intuitive bond with his or her student…Integration…The first yoga session with a new student is devoted exclusively to establishing channels of communication for this bonding process to take place."[35] We at LAM call this integration the creation of the "safe space" where you are connected energetically to the child and have established a positive reciprocal energy flow between the parent, professional and child. Ms. Sumar further states, "At this early stage, the sensory contact of massage is an excellent way to begin bonding and integration."[36] She even has a detailed picture description of each of the "preparatory stage exercises" of yoga therapy for this age group.[37]

Ms. Sumar describes the next stage of development as the "Inductive Stage or Initiating Asanas" for children from 6 months to one year old. We at LAM believe that once the safe space is established, it is then possible to begin initiating playful and passive movement between parent, professional and the child. In addition, there is an excellent illustration of all sixteen yoga poses used for this "Inductive Stage" in her book.[38]

Following the Inductive stage is the "Interactive Stage" where Ms. Sumar is "boosting the level of participation" for children one to two years of age" who can "sit alone" and "stand or walk with a minimum of assistance."[39] LAM believes that once children are able to follow one-step directions and exhibit appropriate gross and fine motor skills, then more complicated levels of yoga movement can be introduced with minimum assistance and maximum cooperation. The well-established "safe space" created in the prior level between the parent, professional and child will facilitate a seamless transition to this level. Also, there are clearly depicted illustrations of the "Interactive Stage" exercises in her book. [40]

After the Interactive Stage comes the "Imitative Stage" that Ms. Sumar says "develops independence" for children ages 2-3 years. During this stage, she claims, "The child needs to have mastered many basic motor and cognitive skills. He/she should be able to stand and walk without assistance, understand your instructions, and imitate your movements." [41] A yoga practice chart containing clear illustrations for the "Imitative Stage" can also be found in her book. [42] For ages 3 and up, she describes "group classes" that have the same basic course outline as the "Imitative Stage" program done with other students in a group setting. [43]

We at LAM highly recommend this book. We used the various yoga techniques described by Ms. Sumar in the LAM program to create and/or maintain the "safe space" necessary for admittance to the "LAM Buffet." We believe that every child with special needs will move at his/her own pace and will pass through each stage at his/her own rate of development. Remember, our slogan is "no one size fits all." At LAM, the stages described by Ms. Sumar were used only as a guide for lesson planning. LAM met each child at his/her own particular stage and moved the child forward in an appropriate developmental manner without judgment or anxiety. There were no tests to pass before entering a particular stage. Once you start to use the "LAM Buffet" strategies, you will know when to move the child forward based on your intuition and clinical observation.

At LAM, we used yoga movement in three distinct ways:

Hands on Approach

The adult modeled the yoga instruction and physically helped the child move safely into a particular pose. Here are some examples of this technique:

In "Mountain Pose" or "Tadasana", the adult stood behind the child while guiding the child into the pose. The adult could then hold the child's hips or feet to ground and center the child. Another example is "child's pose"/ "turtle pose" or "balasana." In this pose, a child assumed the position of a crouched turtle. The adult squatted or knelt behind the child holding both sides of the child's hips. In "cobra pose"/"snake pose" or "bhujangasana," the child was on his/her belly. The child lifted the head, neck and shoulders up with the forearms while the adult put light hand pressure on the child's ankles to ground the feet.

Family Yoga

The parent and the child were positioned on parallel mats either joined or slightly separated. Both followed the professional's instructions and visual model of how to perform the yoga pose. This particular type of yoga practice was for the developmentally more advanced child. It is the format of a "typical" family yoga class run at yoga studios. The difference here at LAM was that the parent was present but was instructed not to make any corrections or judgments about the child's performance. The parent engaged in the activity with the child on a level-playing field. This is extremely important to note since the LAM program did not want any negative energy to flow between parent and child. The child felt empowered and safe simultaneously during a LAM session. The focus here was always on the creation and maintenance of the safe space by the LAM practitioner.

Partner Yoga

The adult and child joined together on the same mat executing various poses as "partners" helping to support each other physically and emotionally in any particular movement. It involved the simultaneous movement into various poses by the two participants. Each participant created physical support for the other in the pose. Like family yoga, partner yoga involved no judgment or correction by the adult and leveled the playing field once again to a higher energetic vibration of trust and love. Here are some examples of yoga poses used during "Partner Yoga":

In "tree/vrksasana pose," the participants, facing in the same direction, linked their arms behind the back of the other participant while standing on one leg. This created mutual balance and support. Each participant knew on some level that the "tree" if not supported by the other would fall. In "Warrior Two/ Virabhadrasana Two," facing away from each other in opposite directions, the adult/child pressed the pinky toe sides of their back feet together while connecting back arms together assuming the Warrior Two pose. There are many other "partner yoga" poses that may be used. For more information, please consult a licensed yoga teacher.

BREATHING INSTRUCTION AND CONSCIOUS BREATHWORK:

We at LAM used breathing practices as a means to ground, center and bond parent, professional and child. Breath work increases the autonomic nervous system's parasympathetic response while decreasing the autonomic nervous system's sympathetic response. In *The Yoga Adventure for Children* by Helen Purperhart, various breathing exercises are described that "can help channel energy and reduce stress and tension." [44] Breath work is an extremely useful tool for both energy types: hyperactive and hypoactive. As mentioned earlier in this chapter, children with special needs feel disconnected from their bodies whether there is too much energy flowing up and out of their heads (hyperactive) or not enough energy flowing at all (hypoactive). In either case, breath work balances the energy of the body.

At LAM, breath work was a valuable modality that could facilitate the safe space necessary for entrance into the "LAM BUFFET." LAM will explore the simplest breathing practices and advance to the more complex ones in our following discussion. There are no specific age requirements for each of these breathing practices. We found it is best to experiment at any age. Use your intuition. Be playful. If a child exhibits a high-level of frustration, try another practice or discontinue.

Basic Child-Centered Breathing Exercises

Kangaroo Breathing

This was the first breathing exercise that we had recommended for parents/caregivers. This exercise fostered energetic bonding, trust and attachment that we felt was so critical to the creation of the safe space at the LAM Buffet.

This practice can be initiated as early as possible and is most effective if it begins in infancy. Sit up or lie down in any comfortable position with the infant/child positioned heart to heart with the parent/caregiver. The parent/caregiver should then try to match their breathing pattern with the child's pattern. This can be done for any length of time. Although the child is too young to be aware of his/her breathing pattern, the union of breathing rhythms between the parent/caregiver and child syncs the child's breathing pattern and elicits the parasympathetic nervous system's response in the child. In addition, the parent/caregiver's nervous system syncs into the parasympathetic mode as well. Another benefit of breath synchronization is the release of oxytocin. "Oxytocin, a neural hormone plays an essential role in bonding and attachment."[45]

Stuffed Animal Breathing

At LAM, we used small stuffed animals and had the child lie with his/her back on a mat while placing the stuffed animal on his/her belly. The child would see the movement of the stuffed animal just from his/her normal breathing pattern. Then, the child was instructed to take a deeper breath so that the animal would move higher. Another version of this exercise was to use a large stuffed animal or teddy bear and place it on the mat first while having the child lie on top of it with the child's belly pressing against the stuffed animal. The child would notice the movement of the stuffed animal as he/she breathed. "Most children aren't usually conscious of their breathing…they will understand the best way to breathe if they can see what they are doing."[46] Both exercises increased the child's awareness of breathing consciously.

Pop The Balloon Breathing

At LAM, we instructed the child to coordinate an inhale with opening of the arms by taking a deep breath in and then closing their hands to "clap" or "pop" the balloon as he/she exhaled while saying "pop." This was an exercise that required understanding of multi-step directions. However, parent/professional can be the guide for the child by actually using a hand-over-hand assist method and proceeding slowly. If the child is sensitive to noise, whisper the word, "pop" instead of saying it loudly.

Bubbles Breath

Either the adult or the child was encouraged to blow bubbles. For children that lacked the prerequisite breathing skills for blowing bubbles, the adult modeled a deep inhalation and exhalation that the child could imitate. We found bubbles to be a very playful and fun experience for all of our children in our LAM Program. This was also an effective oral motor play therapy tool that developed the obicularis oris muscles or lip muscles necessary for speech sound development.

Cotton Balls Breath

This was another effective oral motor play therapy tool as well as an effective breathing practice. Cotton balls were placed on the edge of a child's mat so that the child could blow the cotton ball off the mat with or without a straw. Other games were used with a cotton ball. For the young child, the adult and child could take turns blowing the cotton ball into a cup. For the older child, the adult and child each could blow their own cotton balls in a competitive race.

Stair Breath

This practice was usually taught to older children. The adult guided the child to inhale little breaths while going up an imaginary staircase. The adult then guided the child to exhale slowly at the top of this imaginary staircase while sliding down an imaginary slide.

Elevator Breath

This practice also was taught to older children. It involved taking a large inhale going up into an imaginary elevator and then exhaling fully as you went down.

Lion's Breath

This practice involved opening the mouth wide while sitting on the heels with knees close together and tops of feet on the floor. The participants were instructed to inhale through the nose and then exhale through an open mouth with a protruded tongue. The participants would then roar like lions. Lion's breath is great for releasing anxiety and stretching the muscles of the face, throat and tongue that are necessary for speech development.

I Love You Breath

The adult demonstrated this breathing practice by inhaling while opening the arms wide. The adult then stated, "I love you" while closing their arms into a self-hugging position.

Sunshine Breath

On the inhalation, the participants started the practice by standing and reaching up for the sun. On the exhalation, the participants brought their arms down to their hearts to capture the sun's energy. This breath would be done 3-5 times in a row.

Bunny Breath

The participants were instructed to breathe like bunnies by inhaling little sips of breath and then exhaling while saying "ahhh" through the mouth. This practice creates relaxation in the body.

QIGONG

Qigong by definition means the integration of gentle body movements, self-massage, breath practice and deep relaxation into a single practice. Roger Jahnke, Doctor of Oriental Medicine, in his book, *The Healer Within* states:

"In China, the integration of these methods is called Qigong (Chi Kung), meaning 'vitality enhancement practice'. In India, it is called Yoga. Both of these Asian traditions of self-healing have been called 'internal exercises', 'moving meditation', or 'meditation in motion'. Taiji (Tai Chi), which is familiar to many Americans and Europeans, is one kind of Qigong."[47]

We at LAM used Qigong for children with special needs and their parents in a typical session to ground, calm and center both the parent and child. We witnessed first-hand the changes from frenetic energy to peaceful energy that Qigong had created in our participants and in the physical space of the session room. The whole room became the safe space.

Often, a typical LAM session began with Qigong. Participants were first instructed to stand in the "preliminary" Qigong posture. This posture required feet hips width apart, the shoulders relaxed and the arms dangling at the sides not touching the body. In this posture, the knees were slightly bent to allow the tailbone to root and to move slightly under the spine slightly engaging the lower abdominal muscles. This would "allow the pelvic bowl to adjust itself so that it is upright."[48] The head was placed directly on top of spine and shoulders. Once this preliminary posture was established, then simple arm movements were coordinated with the breath. Typical postures used during a LAM session were the following: 1) Stand in the preliminary posture and breathe in and out deeply in a rhythmical manner about 4-5 times and then return to a normal breathing pattern. (2) Stand in the preliminary posture, move the arms up during the inhalation and exhale while moving the arms down. (3) Stand in the preliminary posture, on the inhalation, raise the right arm up. Bend to the left while exhaling. Return to the standing position while inhaling. Exhale and bring right arm down to side. On the next inhalation, raise left arm up. Bend to the right side while exhaling. Return to the standing position while inhaling. Exhale and bring left arm down to side. Repeat this 4-5 times. This exercise stretches out the side body or oblique muscles. (4) Stand in the preliminary posture, inhale and bend at the knees while cupping hands forward and reaching up as if scooping up water. Then, exhale and pretend to pour the water all over the body. The intention is to bathe yourself with Qi or energy. There are many more Qigong exercises that combine gross motor skills with breath similar to yoga movement.

If the child could tolerate touch, parents would use "massage" for the child's hands, feet or ears. Massaging the hands, feet and ears is a very calming experience and energetically bonded the parent/caregiver with the child in a loving and joyful manner. Qigong usually comprised 5-10 minutes of a typical 45 minute LAM session. For more information, we recommend the book, "*The Healer Within*" by Roger Jahnke.

Guided imagery and visualization may be used during Qigong movement practice as well as during yoga practice. LAM found this combination to be very effective. The use of these techniques made the session more fun and playful for all participants. Some common examples: reaching for the sun, bathing with water, bending like a tree in the wind, and having a dragon's tail. If you decide to use some Qigong or yoga practices, let your imagination guide you and trust your "inner knowing".

Again, if you encounter extreme frustration or resistance with any of these Qigong practices, please discontinue their use and perhaps re-introduce at a later time. Remember that the safe space must be maintained at all times and never compromised. This is the very reason why the LAM Buffet allows the practitioner to choose from many different modalities.

MINDFULNESS TRAINING

Mindfulness training is one of the cornerstones of the LAM non-traditional therapy modalities used in the LAM program. At LAM, mindfulness training involves the willingness to sit quietly and focus on the present moment. As described in Chapter 3, for adults, mindfulness involves just being quiet and aware while doing mantra, breath work, and/or visualization while meditating. For children, sitting still is usually unattainable unless they are involved in another activity. LAM created the proper environment for mindfulness to occur by structuring LAM sessions in a playful way that would relax the physical body and calm the sympathetic nervous system of the child. Through the use of playful games, yoga movement, breath work and meditation strategies, the safe space necessary for mindfulness was created. Once this happened, the LAM professional could instruct the participants to use the different types of mindfulness training.

Mantras/Affirmations

At LAM, both mantras and affirmations were used interchangeably with children and their parents. A mantra is defined as a word or group of words strung together to be said aloud or quietly over and over again. Mantras are used to give the mind something to do while the child can sit quietly and go inward. It has grounding, centering and balancing properties for the mind, body and spirit. At LAM, any positive word or words could become a child's mantra. The child could even make up his/her own mantra. Affirmations are defined as statements that provide emotional support and encouragement. They are used to give positive feedback to the mind, to create positive thought patterns and to empower the child. They don't necessarily have to be repeated as often as a mantra and do not have to occur during a quiet time. However, they could be repeated as often as necessary to create the positive result or be said during a quiet time.

Examples of one-word mantras are "peace", "love", "joy" and "happy". Some common examples of affirmations are: "I can do it", "All is well", "I am peace", "I am love", and "I am strong".

Mudras

At LAM, mudras or hand-positions were used to facilitate energy flow in the body in order to ground and center. They are excellent for developing fine motor coordination and can be used playfully during finger play songs or during mindfulness training. During Mindfulness Training, the use of mudras encourages attention to task and staying present. Three examples used often during Lam sessions are: 1) the pressing of the thumbs against the pointer fingers with the hands resting gently on thighs; 2) the pressing of the hands in prayer position at heart center, and; 3) the pressing of the base of the hands together while opening the fingers into a flower shape at the throat.

More complex mudras involve changing the hand or finger position while repeating a mantra or affirmation. The one we used at LAM very often is called, "I can do it." This involves the pressing of the thumb against the pointer finger while saying "I", pressing of the third finger against the thumb while saying "can", pressing the ring finger against the thumb while saying "do", and lastly pressing the pinkie finger against the thumb while saying "it". If the child can master the use of both hands, that is the preferred method. For more information on mudras and their use, please consult a licensed yoga teacher. Mudras are very useful. However, if the child experiences extreme frustration and resistance due to delayed fine motor skills, then move on from this task and try at a later time.

Meditation strategies

Meditation strategies for children usually involve some form of conscious play. When children are engaged in conscious play or in a play activity in a mindful way, LAM believes that meditation is occurring. This type of play creates an unrestricted energetic flow for all participants. We observed during LAM sessions that LAM energy work during these meditations helped create the necessary positive energetic connection between the parent, child and professional. The LAM acronym - "Love, Acceptance Matters" that occurred during meditation maintained the safe space necessary for the child's growth and development.

In a typical LAM session, meditation involved letting go of all resistance and just being open to the present moment in a fun-filled, joyful way. This happened because the authentic selves of all participants were more present during the activity (See Chapter 3 for definition of authentic self). During LAM sessions, we observed that a meditative state had eliminated the aforementioned negative play behaviors that could lead to tantrums or meltdowns. It was so wonderful to witness a fun and loving exchange without worry about judgment or outcome.

At LAM, we used many simple everyday activities in a very mindful way to create a meditative state. The only restriction was for the parent not to instruct, reprimand or correct their child unless there was a safety concern. Our mottos during play were "Surrender," "Go with the flow" and "Find your own inner child." Here are some examples of LAM meditation strategies used for children:

LAM Walking Meditations

There are many types of LAM walking meditations that we adapted for use. Walking meditations are particularly useful for grounding and centering. At LAM, all the participants walked around the therapy room slowly landing on colored plastic discs. Sometimes, soft music played in the background. The pattern of the discs could stay the same or change to create more attention to this task. The children could play "stop" and "go" on a disc similar to the "red light green light game" or "freeze game" depending on their cognitive level. During these games, expressive language skills would be stimulated and practiced by allowing the child to request the particular game or signal in the game. All participants could walk backwards and forwards without discs or side-to-side. All of these games fostered an awareness to be present in the moment. Any walking play activity that is chosen can be done in a meditative manner. Use your own creativity and follow the child's lead.

LAM Heart-Centered Meditations

The aim of LAM heart-centered meditations was to connect energetically the hearts of the participants in a loving, nurturing and peaceful way. LAM believes as do Eastern philosophical traditions that the "heart center" or "spiritual heart" is the place where feelings reside and is the home of the "True" or "Authentic Self" (See Chapter 3 for definitions). For LAM purposes, it was very important to move energy from the "head" or thinking brain to the "heart" or spiritual self for all participants in our program. The heart center holds the higher energetic vibrations of unconditional love, innate harmony, compassion and truth. LAM believes that if the heart center dominates, then love and acceptance will take precedence over worry, fear, guilt, anger and shame. This can be achieved through the use of many different types of heart-centered meditation strategies:

LAM Heart to Heart Meditation (Kangaroo Breathing Practice)

The parent sat behind the child and pressed his/her heart center into the back of the child's heart center. Parent attempted to merge his/her breathing pattern with that of the child's. This worked especially well for very young children.

LAM "I Love You" Heart Meditation

Both parent and child were seated on the same mat. The parent sat behind the child and placed his/her hands over the child's hands. The parent brought the child's hands to the child's heart center while saying "I love you" aloud. If child was verbal, then the child would join in with the affirmation.

LAM Traditional Heart Meditation

The child and parent were seated on parallel mats. Each participant pressed the palm of his/her right hand on his/her own heart center and pressed the left palm on top of the right hand with the thumbs touching each other. This meditation could be combined with the use of sound therapy (e.g. "yam"- Sanskrit seed sound for heart chakra) or a mantra or affirmation like "I love you" or "peace". This meditation could also be combined with the use of conscious breathing practices such as "Elevator Breath"(see earlier in this chapter).

LAM Back-to-Back Heart Meditation

The parent and the child were seated back of heart to back of heart with elbows locked. The aim of this meditation was to synchronize the breathing patterns of each participant into one breathing pattern. The participants were instructed to visualize the breath as entering and leaving both hearts at the same time. This was usually practiced for children developmentally ten years of age or older since it involved more advanced cognitive skills.

LAM Grounding Meditations

LAM Grounding meditations overlap with many of the other types of meditations and breathing practices that we have already described. A LAM grounding meditation is defined as any meditation practice that mindfully brings the energy down into the feet or towards the ground. LAM grounding meditations can be active or passive.

LAM active grounding meditations are the following:

Mindful Marching

Some children with special needs are "toe walkers" whose feet do not fully engage with the floor. Marching mindfully with or without plastic discs on the floor helped the child to ground the whole foot to the floor. Music was played according to the particular sensory needs of the individual child.

Cobra Meditation

While on parallel mats, the participants were prone. They were instructed to raise the head, neck and shoulder with arms at chest level while pressing their hands into their mats and hiss like snakes.

Hotdog Meditation

The child would lie across the mat at one end perpendicular to edge. The child was then rolled up in a mat and rolled across the floor and unrolled. The parent and/or professional were encouraged to incorporate any other pretend play or speech modeling activity with this meditation.

LAM Passive Grounding Meditations are the following:

Restorative Yoga Poses

Restorative yoga poses typically use "props" to support the body in a particular posture for relaxation. The professional guided the participant to experience a meditative state while in various postures such as Corpse Pose, Legs Up the Wall Pose, and Child's Pose. For more information, consult a licensed yoga teacher.

LAM Guided Visualizations

In the LAM program, guided visualizations for children were synonymous with pretend play. Children with special needs often have a difficult time engaging in pretend play. Most of these children needed modeling and direct instruction in how to pretend appropriately. We found that the LAM Energy work had facilitated guided visualization or pretend play. The parent/professional was guided to play with the child in an imaginary manner with hand puppets, a toy kitchen, picnic foods and utensils, a doctor's kit, stuffed animals, etc. energetically transmitting peace, grounding and nurturing through focused intention. This would trigger the parasympathetic nervous system's response and result in a relaxed state for the child. Once the child was in this very safe and nurtured space, the child was able to engage purposefully in pretend play. We were privileged to witness the remarkable spontaneous emergence of pretend play skills in children who had lacked them prior to LAM sessions. For many years, traditional therapy techniques had been used with these children with no successful outcome.

CASE STUDY NUMBER 7:
DAVID D. AND KRISTEN

David was a four-year-old boy who came to LAM after two and a half years of receiving Early Intervention and subsequent specialized therapy services in a self-contained preschool class in the district in which he lived. He was diagnosed with mild autism spectrum disorder with deficits documented in the areas of pretend play and social skills. During David's first LAM session, it was observed that he was unable to imitate frequently observed activities in simple pretend play or guided visualization sequences. For example, he was unable to imitate feeding a doll during a "pretend picnic". He could not initiate a conversation that was relevant to himself and the listener. In addition, he exhibited stereotypical and obsessive interest in certain games or action heroes and was inflexible with the types of play offered in a typical LAM session. Much to everyone's joy and amazement, during the third LAM session, David made a breakthrough in both pretend play and social skills. He was able to role-play for the very first time using a pig puppet and a "Scooby Doo" puppet and even used different inflections in his voice to denote the characters he was depicting. Spontaneously, he began asking and answering yes/no questions appropriately and was able to initiate a conversation with the adults present in the room. It is important to note that LAM Energy work by intention was being used during all of these sessions. It is LAM's belief that David's breakthrough occurred with the combination of LAM Energy work and the use of the non-traditional "LAM Buffet" modalities.

Therefore, *we can't emphasize enough how important Mindfulness Training is for parents, professionals and children with special needs.* Mindfulness Training facilitates the creation of a "safe space" so that all participants can experience the parasympathetic nervous system's response while changing the paradigm from "fixing" to "supporting." Mindfulness Training practices allow peace, joy, love, trust and acceptance to be experienced. The goals of the LAM Mindfulness practices are to be fully present, happy, and peaceful. When this occurs, time doesn't appear to exist since there is no space for past memories of pain or for future worries. Everyone can finally sigh with relief "AHHH" and relax by just being present.

SOUND THERAPY/MUSIC THERAPY

Albert Einstein (1879-1955) said, "If I were not a physicist, I would probably be a musician. I often think in music. I live my daydreams in music. I see my life in terms of music."[49]

We at LAM believe that sound therapy/music therapy can be strongly effective in creating and maintaining the safe space for children with special needs, parents and professionals. Traditional music therapy for children with special needs has been very effectively used since the 1950s and 1960s with great success in decreasing self-stimulation behaviors, meltdowns, and hyperactivity while increasing attention, ability to follow directions and intentional communication. We at LAM used sound therapy/music therapy as one offering on our "LAM Buffet" table. We have chosen to discuss it here as a non-traditional therapy modality because most of the time we used it in a non-traditional manner. However, sometimes it was included as part of sensory therapy (traditional modality) of the LAM program.

During LAM sessions, sound therapy/music therapy was used to facilitate different energetic reactions from our clients. LAM might use fast-paced energetic music to increase and synchronize our clients to a higher level of energetic vibration and slow, gentle music to decrease and synchronize them to a lower level of energetic vibration. In each case, music facilitated the change in the inner energy level of our clients so that either a joyful, happy vibration or a grounded and centered vibration could be created. This allowed for greater receptivity to the LAM Energy work.

"Sound healing uses the power of sound and vibration to restore one's body, mind and spirit to a sense of balance and harmony… Indigenous cultures all around the globe understand this and have used some form of sound healing since the beginning of time. Sound Healing has begun to resurface in the modern world and is rapidly finding its way into hospitals, clinics and hospice centers as a powerful means of promoting health and wellbeing. Sound Healing techniques vary but all involve the application of sound waves and harmonic vibrations to the physical and subtle bodies through the use of instruments including the human voice."[50] Dr. Masaru Emoto (July 22, 1943- October 17, 2014), a Japanese author and international researcher and entrepreneur claimed that human consciousness has an effect on the molecular structure of water. In his book entitled, *Messages From Water*, one can view Emoto's results that depict how ice crystals are changed by emotional energies and vibrations. His water crystal experiments consisted of exposing water in glasses to different words, pictures or music, and then freezing and examining the aesthetic properties of the resulting crystals with microscopic photography. Emoto stated, "…a beautiful array of crystals…is formed when natural water is exposed to beautiful music" and non-aesthetically pleasing crystals are formed when exposed to discordant music or negative words."[51] His results have been well documented but not repeated by other scientists.

Although the conventional scientific community has called his work "pseudo-science", at LAM, we consider Dr. Emoto's work invaluable. LAM believes Dr. Emoto's premise that vibrations affect physical matter is correct. In fact, LAM Energy work is based on this very premise that energy is transferred by intention (See Chapter 2). The transfer of positive energy between parent, professional and child is the cornerstone of the creation of the safe space at the "LAM Buffet". During LAM sessions, we had successfully used sound/music therapy during Mindfulness Training. In fact, sound/music therapy could be utilized during yoga movement practices, breathing practices, qigong and during the use of traditional therapy modalities. Sound/music used in LAM sessions may have included but was not limited to the following: (1) softly played new age music; (2) nature sounds; (3) drumming; (4) repetition of Sanskrit sounds such as "lam, vam, ram, yam, ham, and om"; and (5) children's music/pop songs.

During a LAM session, a synergistic effect was created by the combination of the sound/music therapy with the LAM Energy work. It is well-known that both traditional and non-traditional sound/music therapy could facilitate the parasympathetic nervous system's response in both the parent and child so that relaxation would occur. By adding the component of LAM Energy work to sound/music, we had observed a much greater connection between the body, mind and spirit of all participants in our LAM programs.

Here at LAM, we witnessed firsthand the dramatic synergistic effect that sound/music therapy combined with LAM Energy work had on our clients. For example, a non-verbal 18-month-old baby who came to see us started to coo and babble immediately after we repeated the Sanskrit sound "OM" multiple times while using LAM Energy work simultaneously (Case study number 2). Another example of this phenomenon occurred when a ten-year old boy with Down Syndrome with limited spontaneous expressive language blurted out, "I love yoga" to both his mom and the LAM practitioner (Case study number one).

In conclusion, LAM believes that when non-traditional modalities are used as described above in conjunction with traditional modalities and LAM Energy work, children with special needs will enjoy a newfound belief in their own capabilities. This will empower them to take steps towards more and more independence in all areas of their development. Without effort, each success will lay the foundation for the next success. As parents and professionals, we can only hope and wish that this would happen for our children in this lifetime. Once this process starts occurring, parents will witness happily all of the transformational growth changes as well as the reduction in negative behaviors in their children. Parents, you can at last relax with your child and start to enjoy the journey to adulthood together.

In the past, many parents had approached us and asked, " How can I deal with my child's overwhelming negative behavior patterns to allow for the type of interaction with my child that LAM describes?" "How can I get my child to your 'LAM Buffet' if I can't even get him to school without a meltdown?" Some parents even had asked, "How do you do this program? It seems too good to be true." We understand your concerns and your frustrations. Please join us in the next chapter for a deeper understanding of these challenging negative behaviors and LAM strategies for managing them.

Chapter 6

Specific LAM Strategies for Challenging Behavioral Situations

LAM's philosophy regarding challenging behaviors and situations is based on this concept: *As a parent or professional of children with special needs, most of us must change the way we react to the negative behaviors of the children.* For parents, a negative event can trigger a reaction that will involve a power struggle with the child. Parents often try to eradicate the negative behaviors by reacting and asserting supreme control over the child. Many times, this only exacerbates an already unpleasant situation and doesn't achieve any lasting positive results. For professionals, negative behaviors of the child with special needs adversely affect the outcome of the therapeutic session. As a professional, you are trained to react in specific ways by using many different "behavioral strategies." Often, professionals find that these mainstream strategies have many limitations. Whether you are a parent or a professional, the LAM program offers you new strategies for dealing with challenging behavioral situations.

Many children with special needs have difficulty in the areas of self-regulation, impulse control, sensory processing, social cues and norms, higher-level executive functions, language skills and the maintenance of appropriate boundaries. As a parent or professional, it is difficult to discern which of these difficulties may have been the initial "trigger" of the negative behavior. Parents and professionals feel compelled to react immediately when confronted with any type of negative situation especially if safety is an issue. However, parents typically allow their own thought patterns of inadequacy as a parent

Specific LAM Strategies for Challenging Behavioral Situations 89

to surface and overwhelm them. This often leads to feelings that may manifest as anger, fear, shame, grief, and guilt. This is a natural reaction to a stressful experience. As professionals, you might feel that since you've been trained to deal with these negative situations as they arise, you question how others will view your competency when the negative behavioral situation manifests and escalates. For either the parent or the professional, we at LAM believe that your "ego" instead of your authentic self is in your "driver's seat." Shifting your operating paradigm from the ego as the driver to the authentic self as the driver will create a much different outcome for you and the child when encountering these negative behavioral situations.

First, when the authentic self is in the driver's seat, judgment and expectations from others mean very little. Since this process requires living from the inside out, one realizes that external standards are based on outward expectations of what is determined to be right or wrong by the society at large. In either case, when you choose to live from your authentic self, you are focusing only on the present moment with love and acceptance detaching yourself from the outcome of the situation. This process will enable parents and professionals to be "observers" to the negative behaviors of the children instead of "ego reactors." In other words, you don't take the outcome of the negative behavioral event personally as your own deficiency whether you are a parent or a professional. Personal and professional successes are not contingent upon the outcome of the situation. In reality, this is not an easy task and must be practiced consistently over time. As the "**observer**", you remove yourself from the power struggle or professional expectations and become the "guide" or "support" to the child. Then, you are able to stay **patient, detached** and **connected** with the child in a loving and supportive manner. Through the use of this LAM practice, as parents and professionals, you will be intending the high vibrational energies of love, acceptance and support to the child. The child will pick up this energetic transfer and respond in a less resistant and more cooperative way. This may not occur initially but over time it will work. We have seen this phenomenon occur time and again with our LAM clients.

Are you ready to accomplish this goal? If so, then you will need to carry the "LAM Virtual Toolbox" with you at all times. At LAM, we call this "toolbox", "**Observe with patience, detach and connect.**"

The LAM Virtual Toolbox consists of 4 "Do's":

1. Do become an **OBSERVER** and not a participant of the negative behavioral event. When you are an "observer", you become the "director" not the "actor" in the "drama" unfolding before you. Before you decide to make any changes, you have to assess the situation.
2. Do stay **PATIENT**, calm, centered and grounded during the negative behavioral event. You decide not to be reactive but to be a source of strength and guidance.
3. Do **DETACH** the child from the aversive trigger. Remove the child from the trigger and ensure the child's own safety. Find a safe space to let the child be alone with his/her feelings and calm down while maintaining a watchful eye. Do **DETACH yourself** from the outcome of the negative behavior. Do not assume the child's behavior is a poor reflection of your parenting/professional skills.
4. Do **CONNECT** with the child in a loving, accepting and supportive manner through a deeper understanding of the cause or trigger of the behavior. When the child is calm and safe, give the child a positive reinforcement. As the parent, a hug, smile or reassuring words would be forms of positive reinforcement. As the professional, verbal praise, smile or a small token of approval would be examples of positive reinforcement.

A quick slogan for you to remember the four "Do's" that you are carrying in your LAM Virtual Toolbox during a behavioral crisis is **"OBSERVE WITH PATIENCE, DETACH AND CONNECT"**. Now, let's examine how this toolbox works for different types of children in difficult behavioral situations.

THE HYPERSENSITIVE CHILD-EXTREME SENSORY SENSITIVITY

This child is hyper-aware of his/her surroundings to the extent that the environmental input creates extreme anxiety and over-reaction to it. He/she is unable to process, integrate or regulate sensory stimuli appropriately which may manifest in any negative behavior pattern (e.g. extreme crying, screaming, head banging, self-stimulation, etc.). Any sensory stimuli can overwhelm the hypersensitive child creating sensory disturbances in any or some of these areas: light, touch, hearing, taste, and smell. To the professional who works with this child, this is described as disturbances in the processing of visual, tactile, auditory, gustatory and olfactory sensations. As the parent, you must be aware that the child feels "attacked" when over-stimulated and experiences extreme pain and fear at some instinctual level. This results in the triggering of the sympathetic nervous system's response that causes a "fight or flight" reaction to the "toxic" sensory stimuli.

USING THE LAM VIRTUAL TOOLBOX FOR THE HYPERSENSITIVE CHILD

First, become an "**observer**" to the situation. Notice the triggers and remove them for the child. **Patiently** intend to be with the child in a loving and supportive manner. **Detach** and remove the child if possible from the aversive trigger. As the parent or professional, detach your ego from the outcome. **Connect** with the child on any level when he/she is calmer and tell the child that you understand how he/she feels and want to make him/her feel better.

CASE STUDY NUMBER THREE
(MIKE A. AND GABRIELLA)

Mike A. came to LAM at three years of age and was hypersensitive to noise specifically to any type of music, loud or soft. He exhibited the negative behavior patterns of holding his hands over his ears, head banging and running uncontrollably. His mother, Gabriella, knew that auditory stimulation was a "trigger" but lacked understanding of how

Mike actually felt when overwhelmed with this type of stimuli that was noxious to his body. She kept trying to "correct" the negative behaviors through physical force, distraction and de-sensitization. These techniques had minimal effect. Mike was unable to focus or become compliant with any task.

The breakthrough moment for Gabriella came when she attended our LAM Mindfulness Curriculum Workshops and experienced the healing gong meditation. This meditation involved a series of gongs that became progressively louder and louder. The other participants of the class felt the healing properties of the sounds that the gongs made while Gabriella felt anxiety, discomfort and distress. She later told us, "I think I know how my son Mike feels." This awareness changed the way she viewed her son's negative reactions to sound stimuli. From that point on, she could **"observe"** her son's behaviors, be **patient** with him, **detach** him from the trigger and **connect** with him on a deeper level of love and acceptance. Gabriella had transformed herself from being a "fixer" to a "supporter" of her son. In subsequent sessions, the LAM practitioners observed improvements in Mike's eye contact, social skills, focus, compliance, individual interaction with his mother and a reduction in self-stimulating behaviors. From that point on, Mike and Gabriella appeared to be enjoying each other's company during our LAM sessions. Smiles abounded when he greeted and said good-bye to the LAM practitioners. Mom became calmer, grounded and more hopeful that her son's development would continue. Mike is now 5 years old and continues to flourish as he rapidly achieves new developmental milestones.

THE HYPOSENSITIVE CHILD-REDUCED SENSORY SENSITIVITY (E.G. DOWN SYNDROME, GENETIC ABNORMALITES)

The hyposensitive child lacks the appropriate sensitivity to sensory stimuli in his/her environment and has trouble processing information through his/her senses. This child is hypo-aware of his/her surroundings to the extent that the environmental input is not strong enough to elicit a response. The hyposensitive child has an under-reactive nervous system and may appear sluggish and inattentive. This child usually requires more stimulation from his/her environment to feel energized and satiated. There is minimal reaction to all or some type of the following sensory stimuli: light, touch, hearing, taste, and smell. To the professional who works with this child, this is described as under processing of visual, tactile, auditory, gustatory and olfactory sensations. As a parent of a hyposensitive child, you may be frustrated that your child may appear unresponsive and often inattentive. You might think to yourself that your child is "tuning you out" on purpose. But, this is not the case. Simple "ADLs" (Activities of Daily Living- eating, bathing, toileting, dressing) tasks become a challenge since it takes more focus for this child to engage and respond appropriately.

The hyposensitive child is incapable of receiving stimuli appropriately. Because of this disconnect with sensory input, the child is not able to exhibit the appropriate response or output. It is not an issue of "won't" but an issue of "can't". The child can't respond appropriately due to disturbances in the sensory input and integration of the input. It's like having the wrong type of charger for your cell phone. It just won't work without power. Due to the child's inability to understand or express a request, the child becomes frustrated and may start to exhibit some of the negative behaviors such as self-stimulation ("stimming"), yelling, screaming, crying or head banging.

Both parent and child are frustrated in this type of situation. Let's see how the "LAM Virtual Toolbox" can help you as the parent take charge and transform the negative behaviors exhibited by the child into a more positive interaction.

USING THE LAM VIRTUAL TOOLBOX FOR THE HYPOSENSITIVE CHILD

First, "**observe**" the child's reactions to the environment. Does the child have the right amount of stimuli to understand your requests? Do you need to add more sensory input in a calm and loving way? Have you broken the task down into its component parts and provided enough cues for successful engagement? Is your request developmentally appropriate for your child's level of understanding? You as the parent must take the strategies and techniques of professionals and be comfortable in their application in daily life. Second, be **"patient"** with the child during the manifestation of the negative behavior/s. Yelling or screaming should be minimized since it only exacerbates a potentially negative situation. Third, **"detach"** the child from the task or trigger that is frustrating to him/her and detach yourself from the outcome of the negative behavior. Fourth, **"connect"** with the child at a soul level. Empathize with the child in a loving and accepting manner.

CASE STUDY ONE:
KEVIN D. AND BETTY

Kevin D. was an 8-year-old boy with Down Syndrome who exhibited overall low muscle tone (hypotonia) and a slightly open mouth posture with a protruded tongue. His mom Betty was very supportive of her son and really wanted her son to move forward in all areas of his development. At the same time, she was anxious and worried about his inconsistent toilet training and meltdowns. The LAM program was the only holistic therapy Kevin had ever tried.

Initially, Kevin exhibited poor eye contact and attention. He had trouble understanding or processing auditory and visual information. He inconsistently responded to questions that were asked of him. At times, it seemed as if he were not fully present in our session room. At that point, his mom Betty would sternly command him to pay attention. She also would provide repeated verbal cues to re-direct him back on task. During one particular session, the LAM practitioners introduced finger play movements while saying the mantra, "I can do it." Kevin had to move his forefinger to thumb while saying "I", third finger to thumb while saying "can", ring finger to thumb while saying "do" and pinkie finger to thumb while saying "it". Kevin was exhibiting difficulty with the task and extreme frustration. He started to have a meltdown. His mom Betty intervened and forcefully told him to "try again." This exacerbated the meltdown even more. At this point the LAM practitioners intervened and demonstrated to mom the use of the "LAM Virtual Toolbox." First, they instructed the mom to become the **"observer"** and not a reactive participant. Second, they told her to be **"patient"** and supportive of her son's frustration. Third, LAM practitioners instructed the mom to **"detach"** Kevin from the activity that was the trigger of the frustration (i.e. "finger play") and detach herself from the outcome of Kevin's negative behavior. Fourth, she was instructed to **"connect"** with Kevin in a loving and accepting manner by understanding how his frustration with the task could manifest as the negative behavior of a meltdown.

At first, Betty exhibited difficulty using the LAM Virtual Toolbox but over the course of three sessions, she became more adept and more confident in its use. She was also witnessing first-hand dramatic changes in her son through her use of this toolbox at home and during sessions. At home, he was more compliant with toilet training and expressive in his spontaneous language skills. During the fifth LAM session, both Kevin and Betty were able to relax together and enjoy each other's company. Kevin spontaneously commented during LAM Energy work, "I love you mom." Instead of being her son's "fixer," she had become his greatest "supporter."

THE OPPOSITIONAL/DEFIANT CHILD- INABILITY TO FOLLOW RULES WITH CLEAR CONSEQUENCES

Oppositional Defiant Disorder (ODD) is defined by the Mayo Clinic "as a child or teen who has a frequent or persistent pattern of anger, irritability, arguing, defiance or vindictiveness toward you and other authority figures."[52] "According to *DSM-5 (Diagnostic and Statistical Manual of Mental Disorders*, 5th Edition) criteria for diagnosis of Oppositional Defiant Disorder (ODD) show a pattern of behavior that: Includes these symptoms - angry and irritable mood; argumentative and defiant behavior; or vindictiveness from any of these categories:

— Occurs with at least one individual who is not a sibling

— Causes significant problems at work, school or home

— Occurs on its own, rather than as part of the course of another mental health problem, such as a substance use disorder, depression or bipolar disorder

— Lasts at least 6 months[53]

Oppositional Defiant disorder is a complex problem. Possible risk factors for ODD include:

— **Temperament**- A child who has a temperament that includes difficulty regulating emotions such as being highly emotionally reactive to situations or having trouble tolerating frustration.
— **Parenting Issues**- A child who experiences abuse or neglect, harsh or inconsistent discipline, or a lack of parental supervision.
— **Other family issues**- A child who lives with parent or family discord or has a parent with a mental health or substance use disorder."[54]

As stated in the beginning of this chapter, children with special needs have difficulty in the areas of self-regulation, impulse control, sensory processing, social cues and norms, higher-level executive functions, language skills and the maintenance of appropriate boundaries. LAM believes that these difficulties can manifest as ODD (Oppositional Defiance Disorder) in conjunction with other diagnoses. Or ODD can be one more symptom in a constellation of symptoms of a particular disorder. For example, we have seen ODD behavior in children who have ADD (Attention Deficit Disorder)/ADHD (Attention Deficit Hyperactivity Disorder), Asperger's Syndrome, Autism Spectrum Disorder, Down Syndrome, Sensory Processing Disorder and Genetic Abnormalities. For LAM's purposes, the "LAM Virtual Toolbox" can be used for any oppositional or defiant behavior in children with special needs. LAM programs for the treatment of ODD involve training the parent in the use of the "LAM Virtual Toolbox" to facilitate positive family interactions. ODD behaviors are extremely difficult to manage and create an immediate power struggle among family members. As stated many times before, the LAM program emphasizes that parents become "supporters" instead of "fixers."

During a typical interaction with the child with ODD, you as the parent may experience extreme resistance and non-compliance from your child even with the most mundane tasks such as eating, bathing, dressing, attending school, etc. As a parent, you think you have only two choices: Choice #1 is to give in to your child. If you pick choice #1, you as the parent will feel powerless and the child will rule the family as "the bully" with no rules or boundaries in place. Choice #2 is to exert control over your child and control the outcome you wish to achieve. Choice #2 appears to be a better option.

If you pick choice #2, then you are a parent ready for "battle" at a moment's notice and feel that you must "win" the "war" at all costs. As a good soldier, you forge into battle with your child at the slightest provocation determined to control the negative situation. Anger and resentment between you and the child increase dramatically. You feel as the parent that you are the "boss" and are "right" and your child is "wrong." These feelings only exacerbate an already very volatile and tense situation. They are energetically transmitted to your child who becomes more defensive, explosive, oppositional and resistant. Like a bomb that detonates, the negative situation explodes with both parties out of control until someone wins. Either you as the parent eventually give in to the child and he/she "wins" or you as the parent exert so much control that the child becomes powerless and you think you "win." We believe at LAM that both choices are lose-lose situations. Don't despair. There is a third choice: the LAM Virtual Toolbox. This will transform the lose-lose situation into a win-win situation for both parties.

USING THE LAM VIRTUAL TOOLBOX FOR THE OPPOSITIONAL DEFIANT CHILD

First, breathe deeply and **"observe"** the child's defiant behavior. Why is the child acting out? What is or are the triggers? Can I remove the child from the triggers? Is the child unsafe? Is the physical environment safe? Is the child at risk for hurting himself or others? In other words, you are assessing the situation in a calm and thoughtful manner. Second, be **"patient"** with your child and don't let your own anger escalate into an explosive response. By managing your own emotions, you are creating the "mirror" for your child to model. Third, **"detach"** your child from the triggers that may involve the removal of your child from his/her present physical environment to a calmer, safer space and "**detach**" yourself from the outcome. Fourth, "**connect**" to your child in a loving and accepting way. Be supportive and understanding that your child is reacting to a "trigger" that has created pain, fear, anxiety and/or overwhelming frustration. Remember that your child lacks the necessary "strategies" or "software" to cope with these triggers. You must become your child's supporter in helping him/her discover the coping strategies.

CASE STUDY NUMBER FIVE: JIM C AND MOTHER ALLISON

Jim C. came to LAM at age eight with the diagnoses of Oppositional Defiant Disorder, Attention Deficit Hyperactivity Disorder and Asperger's Syndrome. Jim's mother Allison is a single parent and has been separated from Jim's father who is bipolar, a drug user, HIV positive and currently incarcerated. At our first LAM session, Jim exhibited poor attention, hyperactivity and impulsivity. Using the LAM "Virtual Toolbox", the LAM practitioners first "**observed**" the interaction of Jim with his mother and how he played with all the adults present in the room. We observed severe agitation and anxiety in Jim when he was not able to control the play situation or when he had to take directions from the LAM practitioners. "**Patiently**" the LAM practitioners instructed mom to refrain from correcting Jim during any of his outbursts during the different play tasks. Third, we educated mom to "**detach**" Jim from the triggers by using the strategy of re-direction during play that would diffuse his negative outbursts and we encouraged her to "**detach**" from the outcome. Finally, we urged mom to "**connect**" with Jim in a loving and accepting manner. At this point, the LAM practitioners made the mother-son connection even stronger through the use of LAM Energy work. After this initial session, Jim remarked to his mother, " I never realized I could be so relaxed and calm before. I feel good."

THE CHILD WITH HIGHER-LEVEL COGNITIVE EXECUTIVE FUNCTIONING DEFICITS (E.G. ATTENTION DEFICIT HYPERACTIVITY DISORDER, ATTENTION DEFICIT DISORDER, ASPERGER'S SYNDROME, HEAD TRAUMA, MOOD DISORDERS)

For our purposes, LAM created this category to illustrate how the LAM Virtual Toolbox can help a child who displays a "mixed bag" of symptoms. In this category, the child may have many different symptoms that may take precedence at different times and in different situations. For example, the child may have been diagnosed with ADHD but also exhibits severe mood swings characteristic of a child with a bipolar disorder. Or a child diagnosed with Asperger's Syndrome may exhibit severe dysfunction in social settings such as school or at home by displaying extreme mood swings and poor social boundaries. Another example is a child with a history of head trauma who may be exhibiting poor attention, impulsivity and poor self-monitoring ability only at school when the task demands are high. There is no "one size fits all" here. This category is broad enough to offer parents a framework for understanding their own child's unique issues but specific enough to offer how the use of the LAM Virtual Toolbox successfully can navigate any challenging behavioral situation.

USING THE LAM VIRTUAL TOOLBOX FOR THE CHILD WITH HIGHER COGNITIVE EXECUTIVE FUNCTIONING DEFICITS (E.G. ATTENTION DEFICIT HYPERACTIVITY DISORDER, ATTENTION DEFICIT DISORDER, ASPERGER'S SYNDROME, HEAD TRAUMA, MOOD DISORDERS)

First, **"observe"** your child during a negative behavioral situation. Notice what behavior is causing this negative behavioral situation. Is it your child's impulsivity? Is it your child's emotional instability to deal with new and challenging tasks? Is it poor attention? Is it the inability to read social cues in peers that causes his/her frustration? Is it emotional dysregulation? Is the child unable to cope with his/her own anger and frustration? Secondly, be **"patient"** and model the appropriate reaction you want your child to see. In other words, don't get caught up in the drama of your child's emotional reactivity. Be calm. Third, **"detach"** your child from the trigger(s) that you have observed and if possible, try to remove your child from the physical environment that is causing the outburst. At the same time, **"detach"** yourself from the outcome. Fourth, **"connect"** with your child as a "supporter" and not as a "fixer."

CASE STUDY NUMBER 9:
ALFRED K. AND BOB (FATHER)

Alfred was a seven-year-old boy who was referred to LAM by his paternal grandmother. He had been diagnosed with ADHD and emotional dysregulation manifesting in aggression and anxiety. He also possessed superior cognitive (IQ of 189-Mensa category) and athletic skills. During the intake of case history, Alfred's grandmother reported that her son was divorced from Alfred's mom since Alfred was three years old. Bob, the father, was the primary caregiver and the paternal grandparents resided in the same home. It appeared from the case history that Alfred had difficulty relating to all members of his family, including his older brother of two years, and his grandparents. In school, he exhibited severe aggression when he didn't get his way. He was extremely competitive to the point of aggression. He tested authority in almost every situation but was most compliant with his father.

The LAM practitioners instructed Bob in how to use the LAM Virtual Toolbox effectively with Alfred. First, we told Dad to **"observe"** the cause(s) of Alfred's negative behaviors. For example, when Alfred refused to comply with a play activity in the LAM session room, instead of saying "no", we gave Alfred two structured choices so that he would not feel out of control. Second, we encouraged Dad to be **"patient"** and not to reprimand the behavior in an authoritative way. Third, we showed Dad how to **"detach"** Alfred from the trigger through the use of controlled choices and **"detach"** himself from the outcome. Fourth, we displayed how to **"connect"** with Alfred in a loving and accepting manner by using Alfred's love of athletics. By making Alfred and his Dad both "members" of the same sports team and the LAM practitioners the "coaches," we were able to facilitate their connection as allies. We only saw Alfred for four sessions, but a lot was accomplished. Alfred and his dad came to a new level of understanding. Alfred's grandmother reported a reduction in Alfred's aggression at home and school. For the first time, Alfred was able to become a member of his family and show appropriate affection. The grandmother tearfully told us, "I am now able to hug my grandson and say I love you."

In conclusion, the LAM Virtual Toolbox can be used for every child no matter what type of negative behavior is displayed. The order in which you use the tools in the LAM Virtual Toolbox is always the same: **Observe** with **Patience, Detach,** and **Connect**. The more you use this "Toolbox", the more proficient you become in knowing how to use the tools. Just like a carpenter knows when to reach for the "right" tool, you too will know in a split second how to proceed when using these tools. Do not despair. Be patient with yourself. Be consistent and persistent in the use of the LAM Virtual Toolbox and you will achieve positive results.

Remember there is an energetic component to the use of this Toolbox. You, as the parent must exhibit confidence in your child that you and your child can get through the challenging situation together and arrive at a positive outcome. This outlook facilitates the transmission of high vibrational energy between you and your child that cannot be underestimated in any interaction. Oprah says it best in the Meditation Series with Deepak Chopra, "Miraculous Relationships": "What you ask for from the world, is exactly what you are getting back."[55] This means that if you send out love and acceptance to your child in the most challenging of circumstances, the child will begin to respond positively. This phenomenon is known as the "Law of Attraction". The "Law of Attraction" states that "like attracts like" and by "focusing on positive thoughts, one can bring about positive results." [56] We at LAM have seen this phenomenon work with many of our children as long as the parent is on board with this philosophy. At LAM, we use the slogan, "Change the parent, change the child." In fact, as our program developed, our

Mindfulness Training Curriculum for parents became a pre-requisite for the child's success in our LAM programs.

As professionals, we implore you to teach your clients' parents/caregivers how to use the LAM Virtual Toolbox. Once you as professionals have incorporated its application into your practice, you will realize its efficacy. Without question, the LAM Virtual Toolbox offers you another wonderful option for managing difficult behavioral situations. It allows you to live in your authentic self rather than in your ego. As a result, you will experience a greater sense of professional and personal satisfaction.

Lastly, the LAM Virtual Toolbox re-creates the safe space for the child.

During any display of negative behaviors, the child is feeling unsafe at his/her core. The child may feel isolated, ungrounded, misunderstood and quite frankly, scared. The Sympathetic Nervous System's response of "Fight or Flight" has been activated. The LAM Virtual Toolbox allows one to **observe** the negative behavioral situation **patiently**. Then, **detach** and **connect** with the child as a supporter to re-create the safe space. This process is very simple to understand yet very profound in its application.

Now that you have read Chapters 1-6, it's time to put on your best outfit and take the child to the "LAM Buffet". At the "LAM Buffet", you can sample whatever will allow love and acceptance to flow in abundance. There are so many possible choices and you can pick and choose as you wish. In Chapter 7, we at LAM are going to illustrate through actual lesson plans how the different choices at the "LAM Buffet" are used to achieve limitless possibilities. Come and join us!

Chapter 7

Sample LAM Lesson Plans

Are you overwhelmed with all this information and don't know where to begin? It's really quite simple. Let's go back to the original LAM Buffet discussed in Chapter One and walk you through using the LAM program at the LAM Buffet.

The LAM Buffet table represents the "safe space" that must be created first. This refers to the physical environment and relates to all of the sensory stimulation that you and your child will process and receive in this space. Higher vibrational energy must exist in this space in order that feelings of love, acceptance, joy, nurturing and support are elicited. Once this "safe space" is created, you will pick up a "plate" which represents your energetic intention of love and acceptance, the LAM Energy Work.

You are now looking at the dizzying array of food choices available on the buffet table. To the left, the foods represent "traditional modalities" that your child has experienced in his/her lifetime. On the right side of the table, are the "foods" that represent "non-traditional modalities" that may be introduced for the first time. How do you know what to choose? Well, first you decide to choose something from the left side of the table. This is a traditional modality/food and it allows you to connect and play with the child in the safe space of the buffet table. Once you've successfully tried one or a few of the traditional modalities/foods, now you are ready to sample the non-traditional modalities/foods from the right side of the table. Offer all the modalities/food choices to the child in a joyful manner and observe the reaction. If the child is receptive to them, then use them in your lesson. If the child resists these modalities/foods, then discard them and pick other modalities/foods until you find the right combination.

These modalities can be used individually in a linear fashion or combined together. For example, you might start playing by rolling a ball back and forth (traditional modality). Then, you may introduce a yoga breathing exercise after you've finished rolling the ball (non-traditional modality). Or you may combine the two at the same time depending on the child's developmental level. Another choice might be to use two traditional modalities before even experimenting with non-traditional modalities. It is important to remember that the child must be compliant with the task and not exhibit extreme frustration.

While these activities are occurring, the parent/professional is able to do the LAM Energy work (i.e."plate"- Chapter 2). The LAM Buffet is unique in that both traditional and non-traditional modalities are used equally. Both modalities are offered on a "plate" of high vibrational energy consisting of love and acceptance. This high vibrational energy is achieved through the use of LAM Energy work. The extraordinary outcome of the meal is the creation of limitless possibilities for both you and the child.

Through the use of case studies whose parents have consented to allow us to use this information, we will present lesson plans that have worked successfully during LAM sessions at Marble Jam Kids®: Center for Creative Arts Therapy and Enrichment in River Edge, NJ. The names of each of these case studies have been changed to protect the privacy of our clients. You may recognize some of these case studies already. We have mentioned some in prior chapters in order to illustrate a particular concept. Here in this chapter, we will describe the lesson plan in its entirety so that you can understand how you can apply these plans to your specific child.

CASE STUDY NUMBER ONE:
KEVIN D. AND MOM BETTY

Kevin D., an eight-year-old boy diagnosed with Down Syndrome, came to LAM with his mom, Betty. He was enrolled in our LAM program weekly for eight non-consecutive sessions. The LAM practitioners had already done a thorough case history intake and learned about Kevin's particular strengths and weaknesses. Kevin was initially shy and had difficulty transitioning into the LAM therapy room. The LAM practitioners created a "safe space"(LAM Buffet table) that was fun and inviting for Kevin. The physical environment minimized any sensory stimulation that could be overwhelming for him. Lights were dimmed. Soft music played in the background. One activity at a time was displayed visually. Kevin entered the room without incident holding onto his mom and then sat down on the floor immediately. The LAM practitioners assessed the low vibrational energy in Kevin's body and began to do the LAM Energy Work ("the plate") that continued for the entire duration of every session. Next, they provided a visual model of walking in a circle to the beat of moderately slow music (two traditional modalities-walking, music). Kevin appeared to enjoy these activities and his energy level increased. The LAM practitioners then introduced playing with a parachute (third traditional modality) where they had Kevin follow 1-step directions and maintain attention and eye contact (fourth traditional modality- speech therapy). Once it was ascertained that Kevin could follow 1-step directions consistently about 80 percent of the time, the LAM practitioners decided to introduce simple yoga movement (first non-traditional modality). The LAM practitioners provided the necessary visual and proprioceptive (awareness of body in space) model. Kevin and his mom participated in this simple yoga movement on parallel mats (asana/movement practice). In subsequent sessions, non-traditional modalities of sound therapy (seed sound "OM"), affirmations/mantras ("I can do it"), mudras and breath work (three part breath) were all introduced as Kevin's level of comprehension improved. There were a total of five non-traditional modalities that were used during our sessions with Kevin.

Over the course of the eight sessions, Betty reported the improvement in Kevin's overall expressive language skills and independence with toilet training. He was so happy to enter the room for the LAM sessions that he couldn't wait for the door to open. He also never wanted to leave when the session was over. Betty's overall level of anxiety lessened dramatically after she had participated in not only her son's LAM sessions but also in the LAM Mindfulness Curriculum Workshops for parents.

Summary of LAM Lesson Plan for Kevin D.:
Creation of Safe Space/ "LAM Buffet Table"
+
LAM Energy Work/ "Plate" at LAM Buffet
+
Traditional Modalities- walking, parachute playing, listening to music, speech therapy
+
Non-Traditional Modalities-yoga movement (asana practice), sound therapy, affirmation with mudra ("I can do it"),
breath work (3 part breathing)
=
Accelerated developmental progress with achievement of new developmental milestones, happiness, joy, love, acceptance, and peace (Limitless Possibilities).

CASE STUDY NUMBER TWO:
KAREN S. AND MOM BARBARA

Karen was our youngest client. She was seventeen months when she first came to see us. She was diagnosed with a genetic abnormality with gross developmental delays and overall low tone. Hypotonia was observed in the core, oral motor musculature and upper extremities. Hypertonia was observed in the thighs and legs. She wasn't able to sit independently, crawl or roll over when we first saw her. Karen wasn't able to differentiate sides of the body but could cross the midline. She exhibited frustration through grinding her teeth and clenching her fists. Karen was receiving Early Intervention that included PT (Physical Therapy), OT (Occupational Therapy) and ST (Speech Therapy). Mom supplemented these therapies with aquatic and chiropractic therapies. Karen was non-verbal and experienced severe delays in feeding skills.

The LAM practitioners first created the safe space for Karen through the use of soft music, low lighting, a soft blanket on the floor and minimal visual distractions. We let Karen stay in her mom's arms and let her get used to her surroundings. The LAM Practitioners observed that Barbara, Karen's mom, had difficulty interacting with her daughter due to the lack of feedback from Karen. We instructed Barbara to interact with Karen in a playful manner without any expectations. At first, Barbara had a difficult time understanding this concept of staying completely present with her daughter yet detached from any outcome (LAM Virtual Toolbox- Chapter 6). The LAM practitioners encouraged Barbara to practice this concept and play with her daughter for brief periods each day instead of searching for new therapies to "fix" her daughter. During the first session, while Barbara was engaging her daughter in discriminate play (traditional modality) with objects (e. g. books, blocks), the LAM practitioners channeled LAM Energy work.

As the sessions progressed over the course of ten months, the complexity of traditional tasks increased. Karen gained proficiency in crossing the midline of her body, grasping and releasing objects, and vocalizing. Reduplicative babbling was emerging. Oral motor and feeding skills were improving. She even started to sit independently and pull up from a sit to stand position and take a few steps with maximum assistance. The clenching of her fists and grinding of her teeth all but disappeared over time.

The only non-traditional modality that was used with Karen and Barbara was LAM kangaroo breathing (see Chapter 5 for details). This breathing practice fosters synchronization of the breath between the child and the parent while increasing an overall sense of well-being and security. Barbara and her husband attended four LAM Mindfulness Curriculum Workshops and had private LAM sessions. Barbara was instructed to use LAM Energy work to deepen her connection of love and acceptance to Karen and began to practice this work daily.

During our time with Karen and Barbara, Barbara experienced a complete transformation in the way she parented her daughter. Barbara was now more aware how her intentions, thoughts and actions could influence her daughter's development. By the end of the LAM sessions, Barbara connected with her daughter at a soul level in a profound way. She became less anxious about her daughter's future and more supportive, loving and nurturing. For the first time, Barbara was able to enjoy more little moments with Karen instead of waiting for the big ones to occur.

In fact, she even described to the LAM practitioners an event that normally would have been extremely distressing. In the past, Barbara would have felt extreme anxiety not only for herself but also for her daughter. This time Barbara used the "LAM Virtual Toolbox." She became the **patient observer** and watched this whole situation unfold **detached** from any particular outcome. She **connected** to her daughter in a more loving and confident way. During this harrowing ordeal, Barbara told the LAM practitioners that she and Karen were a "team." The outcome of this event was that after many hours with no meltdowns from Karen, the distressing situation finally resolved itself.

Summary of Lesson Plan for Karen S.:

Creation of Safe Space/"LAM Buffet Table"

+

LAM Energy Work/"Plate" at LAM Buffet

+

Traditional Modalities- listening to music, speech therapy, discriminate play, physical therapy

+

Non-Traditional Modality- LAM kangaroo breathing

=

Accelerated developmental progress with achievement of new developmental milestones, happiness, joy, love, acceptance, and peace (Limitless Possibilities).

CASE STUDY NUMBER THREE:
MIKE A AND MOM GABRIELLA

Mike A. was a three year eleven month old boy who came to LAM with the diagnoses of Autism Spectrum Disorder and receptive/

expressive language disorder. He was nonverbal and exhibited extreme self-stimulation behavior such as covering of his ears, spinning and running into walls. Severe sensory processing issues were present for auditory and visual stimulation. He lacked eye contact, attention skills and understanding for 1-step directions. The LAM practitioners observed poor play skills. Mike was unable to play discriminately with objects such as blocks or legos. Instead of stacking, he would line up the blocks or legos in a rigid linear pattern. Joint attention and socialization skills were non-existent. Behavioral meltdowns were a frequent daily occurrence according to mom, Gabriella.

The LAM practitioners decided to eliminate all sensory stimulation from the session room in order to create the safe space for Mike. Lights were turned off. The room was silent. A few blocks were displayed in a group in a corner on the floor. During that first session, Mike had to be dragged in by his mother into the session room due to poor transitioning skills. Once in the room, Mike began to run and thrash his body from wall to wall. Mom had to use force to hold Mike back from doing this. The LAM practitioners followed Mike and his mom around the room chaneling LAM Energy work (See Chapter 2). This eventually calmed Mike enough so that he was able to sit with his mom on the floor. The LAM practitioners decided to use the traditional modality of discriminate play with blocks and legos for many sessions. Eventually, other toys such as stickers and bubbles replaced the blocks and legos. While he was playing with his mom, the LAM practitioners concentrated on using LAM Energy work in order to ground, center and reduce his frenetic energy.

Progress was minimal at first but by the end of the tenth session, the non-traditional modality of LAM kangaroo breathing was introduced. After the tenth session, mom reported marked improvements in toilet training and feeding skills. While she excitedly told the LAM practitioners that Mike had only one toileting accident that week, the LAM practitioners were observing Mike drinking from a sippy cup quietly while seated at a table. Mom was astounded at this and tearfully reported that this was the first time she had ever witnessed this behavior.

She told the LAM practitioners that normally Mike would "eat and drink on the run." In addition to all of these behavioral developments, Mike had made a sudden improvement in the area of intentional communication that had been observed by his school speech therapist and classroom teacher.

As the months progressed, Mike continued to make marked improvements in eye contact, social interaction skills, and a reduction in the frequency of meltdowns and self-stimulation behaviors. Therapists at school continued to report accelerated achievement of developmental milestones. One of Mike's occupational therapists at school asked mom, "What's going on that's different here?" Mom happily replied, "A new type of treatment with some energy work." The therapist said, "Whatever it is, keep it going!"

After two years of LAM sessions with many breaks, Gabriella learned how to channel LAM Energy to ground, nurture and support her son. She attended two of our Mindfulness Curriculum Workshops and gained insight into her own negative beliefs and conditioned thought patterns. As stated earlier, she even gained a new sense of compassion for her son's sensory issues for auditory stimulation when she herself reacted adversely to gong therapy during one of these workshops. She said, " Now I know how Mike feels when the sound gets too loud. The gongs made me feel like I wanted to crawl out of my skin." She noticed she was alone in this observation as the other participants of the workshop enjoyed the gongs and felt relaxed.

Mike achieved many developmental milestones over the two years that he received LAM sessions. He started to point and vocalize to express his wants/needs. Improvements in joint attention, eye contact and appropriate social smiling were noted and observed by all the professionals who were working with him. He started to do the gesture "High 5" with the LAM practitioners, use single words such as "ball, up, more, down, and gimme" and even two word phrases such as "Hey Lisa, my turn, no more." Mom reported that empathy was increasing when Mike showed signs of missing his dad when he was away on business. Self-stimulation behaviors almost became non-existent. The frequency and duration of meltdowns drastically reduced. Compliance improved dramatically and Mike had become completely independent with the activities of daily living of feeding and toilet training. His fine motor skills were improving for coloring and drawing as well as for the understanding of simple 1-step directions (e.g. "give me"). Mom reported to us at the last session, "Almost every night I work with Mike using the techniques you taught me. We continue to see gains in language and overall connection to the world around him."

Summary of the Lesson Plan for Mike A:

Creation of Safe Space/"LAM Buffet Table"

+

LAM Energy Work/"Plate" at LAM Buffet

+

Traditional Modalities- discriminate play (blocks, legos, stickers, bubbles), speech therapy

+

Non-Traditional Modality- LAM kangaroo breathing

=

Accelerated developmental progress with achievement of new developmental milestones, happiness, joy, love, acceptance, and peace (Limitless Possibilities).

CASE STUDY NUMBER FOUR:
ANDREW H. AND FAYE

Andrew H. was a nine-year-old boy who was referred by another professional. He had no official diagnosis but mom reported a positive case history for pre and post-natal complications. At eight months gestational age, no movement was observed in utero. Delivery was an emergency C-section at thirty-seven weeks due to poor oxygenation and breech positioning. Faye reported that he currently had poor attention skills, poor expressive language, poor math skills, allergies, food sensitivities, anxiety, reduced impulse control with the presence of meltdowns and poor social skills. Mom literally was crying to the LAM practitioners during the intake of the case history. She said her life with Andrew was a "constant battle." Andrew resisted initiating and completing homework and activities of daily living. He was also bullied at school. Mom was desperately searching for a solution to help her son. We saw Andrew for a total of four individual weekly sessions and his mom for a total of two private sessions. Mom also attended two of our Mindfulness Curriculum Workshops.

At the initial session, the LAM practitioners met Andrew and felt an immediate disconnection between the mom's report and what was actually being observed. At first, Andrew exhibited poor eye contact but was compliant and answered simple questions. Adrienne Murphy, the LAM practitioner who is a licensed speech pathologist, used traditional speech therapy tasks to assess his expressive language and auditory processing of various types of questions. Structured memory games were used to assess both short and long-term memory. To the delight of mom and the LAM practitioners, Andrew excelled on all of these tasks and scored above age-level in his responses. During this first session, the LAM practitioners also introduced various board games to assess his math skills. He was able to follow 3-step directions involving multiplication and subtraction. Once again, he scored well above age-level in this area. It appeared that as the session progressed, Andrew became more and more comfortable as mom relaxed and the interaction with the LAM practitioners continued. During this time, the LAM practitioners were creating a safe space by channeling LAM Energy work to ground, center and nurture both Andrew and his mom, Faye.

Andrew started to smile about halfway through the initial session. The LAM practitioners then introduced "puppet play" to assess pretend play and socio-emotional skills. Once again, Andrew responded in a manner that was inconsistent to his mom's report. He demonstrated excellent pretend play skills and an empathy with the puppets that was extremely advanced for his chronological age. The LAM practitioners also discovered through the puppet play that Andrew loved to draw superheroes. This passion was used to connect with him in the next three sessions.

During the remaining sessions, non-traditional modalities were added to the mix of traditional modalities. Pretend play/guided visualization and affirmations/mantras were introduced to reduce Andrew's anxiety level. The mantra, "I can do it" was taught to Andrew in conjunction with the use of hand movements (i.e. mudra). Andrew told the practitioners that he was using this mantra in school before taking exams to reduce his anxiety level and it worked. Partner yoga with his mom was introduced to foster a loving, supportive connection between them. The LAM practitioners taught Andrew and his mom the breathing practice called three part breath. This breathing practice fostered Andrew's self-empowerment and self-control while reducing his anxiety level. Mom reported that this practice also worked well for reducing her anxiety.

By the last session, both Andrew and his mom were on the same team. The energetic exchange between both of them had changed from resentment, anger, fear, guilt and shame to love, acceptance and support. Mom reported incredible inner transformations for herself in how she related to her family and her son. She reported to us that her son had made "amazing strides" in compliance with everyday tasks and homework and had made a few new friends in school. The LAM practitioners believed that in this case Faye's transformation facilitated the transformational changes in her son. Faye's own negative beliefs and conditioned thought patterns of blame and guilt over her son's difficult birth were transformed into love, hope and support for her son's journey. This case study is a clear example of one of our LAM mottos, "Change the parent, change the child."

Summary of the Lesson Plan for Andrew H:

Creation of Safe Space/"LAM Buffet Table"

+

LAM Energy Work/"Plate" at LAM Buffet

+

Traditional Modalities-speech therapy, cognitive therapy with games, puppet play

+

Non-Traditional Modalities- pretend play/guided visualization, affirmation/mantra/mudra- "I can do it", partner yoga, three part breath

=

Accelerated developmental progress with achievement of new developmental milestones, happiness, joy, love, acceptance, and peace (Limitless Possibilities).

CASE STUDY NUMBER FIVE:
JIM C. AND MOM ALLISON

Jim C. was an eight-year-old boy diagnosed with Asperger's Syndrome, Attention Deficit Hyperactivity Disorder and Oppositional Defiant Disorder. He had severe life-threatening allergies to shellfish and mustard requiring an EpiPen. He had no physical limitations and was currently on a psycho-stimulant medication to increase his attention skills. He experienced severe side effects from the medication that included tantrums, insomnia, and non-compliance. We treated Jim for eight weekly sessions.

Jim's mom, Allison, was a single mother. Jim did speak to his father by phone or Skype everyday. Allison reported that Jim preferred solitary, egocentric play with difficulty sharing or compromising with his peers. Jim was expelled from the aftercare school program at his school for poor behavior. Allison also reported that Jim had difficulty with boundaries and often invaded others' personal space.

Allison was at her wit's end with her son. She didn't know how to handle him effectively and often used ineffective behavioral therapy of reward and punishment. Her son responded to her in kind by embarrassing her and not acting appropriately in social situations. Mother and son were clearly engaged in a "power struggle." During the case history intake, Allison requested that the LAM practitioners help Jim with coping strategies, social problem solving and understanding personal space/boundaries. She had exhausted all traditional therapy options and came to the LAM program receptive to holistic health practices.

During the first session with Jim, the LAM practitioners observed Jim's high level of energy and inability to focus on any structured task. They used the traditional modalities of rolling in a play tunnel, parachute play, and exercise ball play while simultaneously introducing LAM Energy work to create the safe space. It was observed that Jim's energy needed to be brought down to his feet. This combination of the traditional modalities and the LAM Energy work calmed Jim down over the course of twenty-five to thirty minutes. His mom, Allison, was stunned and overjoyed by what she had witnessed. Now, more quiet tasks were introduced to Jim. He started to engage in pretend play (non-traditional modality of guided visualization) with a stuffed animal that was "injured" by placing bandages all over the stuffed animal's body. By the end of the first session, the LAM practitioners introduced another non-traditional modality of yoga called "Corpse Pose" or "Savasana" where mom and Jim were supine on parallel yoga mats. The LAM practitioners channeled more LAM Energy work to both mother and son to foster a greater loving connection between the two of them. Once the session was over, Jim commented, " I never felt so relaxed before!" Mom also experienced complete relaxation during that initial session.

During subsequent sessions, more traditional therapy modalities were introduced (e.g. ball games, weighted blanket, scooters, interactive games) as well the non-traditional modalities of yoga movement, breath work, mantras/affirmations and Qigong. Jim and his mom were taught a simple yoga movement sequence that was very grounding that included the following poses: cobra pose, child's pose, cat/cow and corpse pose. Both were able to execute the following breathing practices: three part breath and back-to-back kangaroo breathing. Jim was able to connect to his own inner confidence with the affirmation/mudra, "I can do it." The Qigong exercise that effectively lowered Jim's energy was the raising of his arms during inhalation and the lowering of his arms during exhalation. During all of these sessions, LAM Energy work created and maintained the safe space for both mom and son.

In conclusion, Jim never exhibited oppositional defiance or meltdowns while in LAM sessions. He usually required twenty to thirty minutes of a sixty-minute session to calm down. Once he settled down, he became compliant and focused on the presented tasks. As Jim calmed down during the LAM sessions, Allison started to relax and began to enjoy this special time with her son. She commented quite frequently, "Coming here is like going to a spa. I feel so relaxed without a care in the world."

In reality, even though progress was made during each of our LAM sessions, there was very little positive carryover present in his home or at school. According to his mom's report, Jim still exhibited poor attention skills, impulsivity, meltdowns, and defiance between sessions. LAM sessions always occurred during a weekend day when Jim was "off" his medication. This was his mom's choice. The LAM practitioners believed that this very choice resulted in the increased amount of time spent that was needed to create the safe space during each session and affected the success of the LAM program for Jim.

Over time, the LAM practitioners believed that real progress could have been made if the medication scheduling had been more consistent. Sessions were terminated after six months. One year later, mom did reach out and try to re-establish an appointment to re-initiate the LAM sessions. At that time, she stated, "This was the only thing that ever worked for my son." However, the sessions were never re-initiated.

Summary of the Lesson Plan for Jim C:

Creation of Safe Space/"LAM Buffet Table"

\+

LAM Energy Work/"Plate" at LAM Buffet

\+

Traditional Modalities- tunnel play, parachute play, exercise ball play, scooter, interactive games

\+

Non-Traditional Modalities- guided visualization (pretend play), yoga movement, three part breath, back to back kangaroo breath, affirmation/mantra/mudra- "I can do it, QiGong

Greater relaxation and compliance, greater bonding between mom and son, reduced anxiety, increased general wellness (Limitless Possibilities).

CASE STUDY NUMBER SIX:
LIAM V. AND MOM VIVIAN

Liam V. was a three-year-old boy referred by his speech pathologist to the LAM program. He was diagnosed with delayed expressive language skills and sensory processing disorder characterized by inconsistent attention, poor self-regulation, meltdown behaviors and tantrums, and oppositional defiance. He was currently enrolled in his district's Special Education Pre-K class where he received occupational and speech therapies.

At the time the LAM practitioners met him, he was undergoing a full GI work-up since he was exhibiting GI symptoms of inconsistent vomiting and diarrhea. Mom tearfully implored that the LAM practitioners "fix" her child by increasing compliance with everyday tasks. She reported that she often "gave in" to him to reduce the frequency and duration of tantrums. She also fervently hoped that his attention skills both at home and at school would increase for all different types of activities and wanted to see a reduction in the frequency and duration of meltdowns when he was told "no." Vivian clearly had a full plate at home with two other children under the age of five and was at her wit's end. We saw Liam for a total of sixteen sessions: eight semi-private and eight private sessions.

At the initial session, Liam exhibited an extremely difficult time transitioning into the session room. Upon entering the room, he clung to his mom while looking down at the floor and biting his cheek. Vivian was clearly anxious that her son was "not behaving well." She was reprimanding her son gently and he retreated further into his shell. The LAM practitioners instructed Vivian to "let him be" and started the session without his participation. Vivian and the practitioners began to walk around the room in time to music and after about five minutes,

Liam seamlessly joined the group with no attention directed at him. During this entire time, the LAM practitioners were channeling LAM Energy work to create the safe space for Liam and Vivian.

After trial and error with traditional modalities (e.g. ball tossing, parachute play, running, jumping), the LAM practitioners found one traditional modality that had immense appeal for Liam. This activity involved the use of brightly colored silk scarves that were first used in simple dance movement. Then, Liam initiated the activity of lying down with them on the floor and instructed his mom to cover him with the scarves.

Since this activity facilitated Liam's parasympathetic nervous system's response, the LAM practitioners realized that this was a perfect sensory activity to create and maintain the safe space. He immediately calmed down and wanted to engage with the practitioners and his mom in pretend play/guided visualization (non-traditional modality). He created his own schema where he was in the "ocean" and the different colored scarves represented both the ocean and the different forms of sea life. His attention, compliance, eye contact and expressive language skills all improved dramatically during this activity with minimal prompts from the LAM practitioners. At the end of this initial session, Liam didn't want to leave the session room. He sat on the floor next to his mom and the practitioners calm, attentive, and smiling. Mom was shocked and overjoyed.

During subsequent sessions, the LAM practitioners introduced more non-traditional modalities: simple yoga movement, kangaroo breathing and sound therapy. Liam was compliant with all of these non-traditional modalities but would always wind up requesting the silk scarf activity.

As positive reinforcement for compliance with Liam's other tasks, the LAM practitioners began using the silk scarf activity in a "clinician-centered" manner whereby the LAM practitioners would determine what type of "game" would be allowed. At first, the LAM practitioners gave Liam two structured choices. This allowed for some sense of empowerment. Liam responded extremely well to this strategy of structured choices and became very interactive. When another child was present during his semi-private sessions, he was willing to become part of the group and to join in the activity. To facilitate carryover of this strategy at home and at school, we instructed Vivian to use this strategy of structured choices. In later sessions, Vivian eagerly reported back to the LAM practitioners that this strategy was working very well.

In conclusion, Liam made moderate progress during the LAM program. However, his physical issues of GI symptoms adversely affected his ability to sustain greater progress over time. We at LAM believe that if Vivian had attended our Mindfulness Curriculum Workshops, she would have been provided with the necessary training to use the "LAM Virtual Toolbox." This would have resulted in a more positive exchange of energy between herself and her son during those challenging behavioral situations she frequently encountered with her son.

Summary of the Lesson Plan for Liam V.:

Creation of Safe Space/"LAM Buffet Table"

+

LAM Energy Work/"Plate" at LAM Buffet

+

Traditional Modalities- ball tossing, parachute play, running, jumping

+

Non-Traditional Modalities- guided visualization/pretend play, yoga movement, kangaroo breath, sound therapy (repetition of "OM")

=

Greater attention and compliance, improved eye contact, improved socialization skills, greater bonding between mom and son, and reduced anxiety (Limitless Possibilities).

CASE STUDY NUMBER 7:
DAVID D. AND MOM KRISTEN

David was a four-year-old boy diagnosed with expressive language delay and elements of autism spectrum disorder including poor social skills, perseveration, rigidity and non-existent pretend play skills. David's mom, Kristen, was very patient, loving, and proactive with helping her son to manage these issues successfully. David had two older siblings. He was referred to the LAM program by his private speech pathologist. During one of the sessions, David's father expressed the desire to have the LAM practitioners help "fix" his son's issues. David was seen for a total of eight sessions consisting of four private and four semi-private sessions consecutively.

During the initial session, David transitioned cautiously and quietly into the session room with his mom. It was apparent that David felt safe and secure in this space as long as his mom was present. There was no need for the LAM practitioners to create the safe space since it already existed between David and Kristen. The LAM practitioners began to channel LAM Energy work at this time. Kristen was smiling, upbeat and eagerly participated with her son walking and singing to the song "Happy." This was the first traditional modality used. David cautiously imitated his mom and the LAM practitioners. He appeared to be totally engaged in the movement but not singing or talking at that time. The other traditional modalities that followed were parachute games, tunnel games, and ball rolling. David was compliant and attentive with appropriate eye contact with these activities as well. Next, puppet play was introduced to foster empathy and pretend play skills.

David would answer concrete yes/no questions presented by the puppet but could not relate to the puppet in a pretend game. He also exhibited a flat affect when the puppet pretended to be sad.

Next, the LAM practitioners used the non-traditional modalities of yoga movement, breath work and sound therapy. During "savasana" or "corpse pose," the LAM practitioners channeled LAM Energy work to a very calm and receptive mother and son. Breath work included "lion's breath." Sound therapy included repetition of the grounding seed sound "LAM."

During subsequent private sessions, David requested the same repetition of activities in the same order that had occurred during the initial session. If the order or type of activity differed from the original session, David got very upset and started to cry. Realizing that this was a problem, the LAM practitioners used the strategy of two structured choices to divert his attention. Kristen just intuitively followed the LAM practitioners' lead. David responded well and transitioned to a new activity without incident. During David's third private session, he had a breakthrough in the area of pretend play/guided visualization. During "savasana" (non-traditional modality), he started to initiate conversation with puppets. He even began to role-play different characters using different vocal inflection with a pig puppet and Scooby doo puppet. It is important to note that the LAM practitioners were channeling LAM Energy work while both David and his mom were in "savasana."

During subsequent semi-private sessions, rigidity in play decreased while pretend play skills emerged. David's social interaction skills with other children kept on improving. He became eager to participate in the LAM activities as either a leader or follower. When the format of the session would change, David would initiate conversation and remind the LAM practitioners what had occurred in prior sessions and then willingly transitioned to a new activity.

Towards the end of his LAM sessions, David spontaneously initiated conversation with the LAM practitioners about a Disney movie that he watched often. He related the story with facts, emotions and songs. Amazingly, David had become a storyteller! He had shifted his perception from the concrete to the abstract. Mom was overjoyed with this revelation.

David's father reluctantly participated in two of the private sessions without his wife. It was clear to the LAM practitioners that there was a different energetic exchange between David and his father. His father was skeptical of the LAM holistic approach and kept asking, "Is this it?" The LAM practitioners re-assured him that all was in perfect order and he begrudgingly accepted this response. During these two sessions, David's father had a positive transformational shift in his perception of his son and his issues. When Kristen returned, she reported to the LAM practitioners, "I never saw my husband so patient and understanding with David as I did after his two sessions with you guys." The LAM practitioners believed that David's father transformed from a father who wanted to "fix" his son according to his own preconceived expectations to a father who was able to release his expectations and support his son in his developmental journey.

In conclusion, David flourished. He was a true success story for the LAM program. He had transformed from being an egocentric and rigid child to a more altruistic and flexible child. Even though David's parents didn't attend our Mindfulness Curriculum Workshops, they learned how to use the LAM Strategies during the LAM sessions. Armed with love and acceptance, both of his parents were now equipped to support his journey.

Summary of the Lesson Plan for David D.:

Creation of Safe Space / "LAM Buffet Table" (already established with the relationship David had with his mom)

$+$

LAM Energy Work / "Plate" at LAM Buffet

$+$

Traditional Modalities- walking and singing to music, parachute games, tunnel games, ball rolling, puppet play

$+$

Non-Traditional Modalities- yoga movement (child's pose, snake pose, corpse pose), breathwork (Lion's Breath), sound therapy (repetition of "LAM"), guided visualization (pretend play)

$=$

Improved socialization skills, improved pretend play skills, improved empathy, improved expressive language, greater flexibility in play, greater bonding between dad and son (Limitless Possibilities).

CASE STUDY NUMBER 8:
GEORGE G. AND DAD, STEVEN

George was a seven-year-old boy referred by his creative arts therapist. He was diagnosed with Autism Spectrum Disorder characterized by overall low muscle tone, inattention, sensory processing disorder,

ODD (Oppositional Defiant Disorder), anxiety, poor eye contact, toe walking, self-stimulation behaviors, perseveration, delayed receptive and expressive language skills, poor socialization skills and poor play skills. The LAM practitioners saw George for a total of eleven private sessions. His father, Steven, accompanied George for ten of the eleven sessions and his mother accompanied him for one of the sessions.

At the initial session, George willingly entered the session room with his father, Steven. The LAM practitioners decided to address gross motor skills and sensory processing issues. Since George demonstrated toe walking and extreme anxiety, the LAM practitioners decided to use the traditional modalities of grounding play activities such as marching, crawling through a covered tunnel and lying underneath a parachute. George was able to follow 1-step directions consistently with minimal cues. During these play activities, the LAM practitioners gave him two structured choices in order to allow him to feel empowered. As the session progressed, George became more compliant and began to exhibit appropriate eye contact. LAM Energy work was introduced during the play activities and was willingly received by both father and son. Both father and son seemed calm and content when the session ended.

During the next three sessions, a tremendous improvement was observed not only by the LAM practitioners in the session but also reported by George's Dad, Steven. Even George's mom, who was skeptical of the LAM program was pleased to see the developmental advances in George. The noted improvements were in the following areas: increased sustained attention, reduced perseveration, increased social interaction, and increased spontaneous expressive language. No meltdowns or negative behaviors (e.g. crying episodes, tantrums) were observed or reported. During the third session, the non-traditional modality of guided visualization/pretend play was introduced with an oversized stuffed animal and puppet (i.e., "Benny Bear" and "Pup in the box" puppet). George responded when playing with the bear, "He needs support." He bandaged the bear's face and mouth with ace bandages. During this time, the LAM practitioners were channeling energy work to release grief and fear in George while he played with the bear and his Dad. George left the session vocalizing loudly but not crying. Dad reported that George continued to vocalize loudly in the car on the way home and that this was a new behavior that had never been exhibited by George prior to the session. During the fourth session, while the LAM practitioners continued to channel energy work, George was even more attentive, compliant and expressive. He said, " I am sad. My heart hurts. I am going to fix my heart" as he bandaged a teddy bear.

During the fifth session, the LAM practitioners noted a regression and only sporadic improvement in George's skills. This session was delayed due to family commitments. At this session, George was unable to follow 1-step directions and initiate spontaneous conversation. He also exhibited high frenetic energy by toe walking, running and perseverating. At this point, the LAM practitioners introduced the non-traditional modalities of breath work (kangaroo breath) and Qigong (massage of hands, feet and ears). These modalities were able to elicit the parasympathetic nervous system's response in George. During that session, the LAM practitioners taught George's father how to use these non-traditional modalities.

During sessions six through eight, George exhibited appropriate attention, understanding and responsiveness. He displayed continued improvement in complex expressive language skills characterized by the use of subordinate clauses and complex sentence structures. He was even able to maintain a conversation for about three turns. During these sessions, while engaged in the non-traditional modality of guided visualization/pretend play, George placed the bandages on himself instead of the bear as he said, "I feel better now."

After a two-month lapse, George returned for the last three sessions with the LAM practitioners defiant and argumentative. He exhibited all negative baseline behaviors and no carryover of any of the above-mentioned skills. The LAM practitioners observed increased toe walking, perseveration and self-stimulation behaviors. Spontaneous expressive language was reduced and utterances were rote and stereotypical. During the last session, George even resisted the channeling of LAM energy work. At this time, George's Dad Steven told the LAM practitioners that he and George could no longer participate in the LAM program due to conflicts within the family. During the progression of LAM sessions, it is important to realize that George's Dad had exhibited a transformational shift. His authentic self had emerged as the "driver." The LAM practitioners suggested to Steven that he and his wife attend the Mindfulness Curriculum Workshops to help support George. Steven and his wife never attended any LAM Mindfulness Curriculum workshops. When George was discharged from the LAM program, his progress had regressed. Today no information is known about how George is doing.

In conclusion, much progress had occurred for George. There was a release of grief and fear from the heart and throat energy centers known in yogic philosophy as chakras. All of George's developmental skills were improving at various times during the LAM sessions. LAM believes that if the parents had attended the LAM Mindfulness Curriculum Workshops more positive and lasting outcomes for George would have occurred. As mentioned earlier, LAM believes "Change the parent, change the child." This is the very reason why LAM made participation in the LAM Mindfulness Curriculum Workshops a mandatory pre-requisite for entrance into the LAM program. Today, all correspondence between the LAM practitioners and George's family has ceased and there is no information available to report on George's developmental progress.

Summary of the Lesson Plan for George G.:

Creation of Safe Space / "LAM Buffet Table" (already established with the relationship George had with his dad)

+

LAM Energy Work / "Plate" at LAM Buffet

+

Traditional Modalities- marching, crawling through tunnel, lying under a parachute

+

Non-Traditional Modalities- guided visualization (pretend play), breath work (kangaroo breath), Qigong (massage of hands, feet and ears)
=
Improved socialization skills, improved pretend play skills, improved empathy, improved expressive language, greater flexibility in play, reduced perseveration, reduced toe walking, reduced self-stimulation behaviors, improved compliance, greater bonding between dad and son (Limitless possibilities).

CASE STUDY NUMBER 9:
ALFRED K. AND DAD, BOB

Alfred was a physically mature seven-year-old boy referred to the LAM program by his paternal grandmother. His grandmother reported that he had ADD (Attention Deficit Disorder) and superior cognitive skills. Although Alfred was never officially diagnosed by his school and didn't have an Individual Education Plan or 504 Plan in place, he had been diagnosed privately. Alfred was currently under the care of a psychiatrist once a month to monitor the administration of his psycho-stimulant medication. He presented with superior size for his chronological age and superior athletic ability. To the LAM practitioners, he looked about ten years old.

Alfred's grandmother was the only adult present during the initial intake. It was disclosed that Alfred's parents had divorced when he was a toddler. He now lived with his father, older brother and paternal grandparents. His mom lived close by and had visitation rights. The grandmother's wish for her grandson was to find "inner peace." According to her report, her grandson "tested authority" and had "trust issues because of the lack of a consistent mother presence." She also described that on Alfred's second birthday, he woke up during a surgical procedure and had suffered nightmares ever since. It was also reported that Alfred exhibited impulsivity, low frustration tolerance, and physical and passive aggressiveness if provoked. The grandmother told the LAM practitioners that there had been many incidents of physical aggression in school that were reported by his teacher. She believed that Alfred possessed poor transitioning skills for low interest activities. Lastly, she explained that Alfred manifested the self-stimulation behavior of picking skin on his fingertips when stressed.

Alfred was seen for a total of four LAM sessions. Alfred's father, Bob, attended the first three LAM sessions while the paternal grandmother and older brother attended the final fourth session. At the initial session, the LAM practitioners' main goal was to develop rapport and trust. Tasks were child-centered vs. clinician-centered. In other words, knowing the history of Alfred's aggression, anxiety and impulsivity, the LAM practitioners tread lightly and didn't cause any power struggles in terms of controlling and directing tasks. Alfred was allowed to determine the activities from all the choices in the session room. This fostered compliance and succeeded in creating the "safe space" for Alfred and his father. They bonded and played well together with no observable conflict. During this first session, Alfred's attention and compliance to task were excellent. No crying episodes or meltdowns were observed. He exhibited good eye contact, good attention and pretend play skills with no transitioning issues. He was very interactive with the LAM practitioners and his Dad.

During the second session, the LAM practitioners focused on structured play tasks that were clinician-centered instead of child-centered. Two structured choices were now used. Again, Alfred's attention, compliance, eye contact, ease of transitioning, and socialization skills were all age-appropriate. No observable negative behaviors occurred. The traditional modalities that were used during the first two sessions were: parachute play, and ball games. The non-traditional modalities that were introduced were the following: guided visualization/pretend play with stuffed animals, breath work and mantra training ("I can do it"). During guided visualization/pretend play and after the breath work and mantra training, the LAM practitioners told Alfred that these practices would help him manage his anger when he felt out of control from not getting his way.

During the third session, the LAM practitioners continued using all the above-mentioned traditional and non-traditional modalities. At this time, the non-traditional modality of yoga movement and partner yoga were introduced. Again, Alfred was attentive and compliant with no observable instances of impulsivity and hyperactivity noted. He was very open and receptive to the LAM Energy work. Bob reported that Alfred had had a "good week" prior to this session in terms of overall compliance and positive behaviors observed by his teachers at school.

During the last session, Bob was not present with his son. Instead, Alfred's paternal grandmother and older brother attended this final session. The LAM practitioners used all the traditional and non-traditional modalities that had been executed in the first three sessions. Alfred exhibited extreme impulsivity, aggression, poor attention, poor compliance, hyperactivity, and extreme competitiveness with his brother that border-lined on bullying. During the yoga movement portion of the session, Alfred set up stuffed animals as a barrier to separate his mat from his brother's mat. Partner yoga was attempted with all three participants but was unsuccessful. After having accepted the LAM Energy work during this final session, Alfred became more compliant and less hostile to his brother. He exhibited this change with the removal of the stuffed animals that had separated his mat from his brother's.

In conclusion, Alfred had made tremendous strides during the first three LAM sessions and regressed during the last LAM session. The LAM practitioners believed that this was no accident. The creation and maintenance of Alfred's safe space depended on his father's physical presence at the LAM sessions because of Alfred's fundamental core issue of abandonment. LAM believed that Alfred's anger was a direct reaction to this core issue. His father was his safe space. Alfred would need much more time to create his own safe space without his father's presence. It is LAM's belief that if Alfred had had more sessions with his father present, he would have been able to arrive at the plateau where he would feel safe enough to create his own safe space. Unfortunately, the

LAM practitioners never had the chance to work with Alfred and his father after these four sessions. However, Alfred did make some lasting progress as evidenced by his grandmother's positive report to the LAM practitioners. She happily shared that her grandson had become more compassionate and loving and less combative towards her and other members of his family.

Summary of the Lesson Plan for Alfred K.:

Creation of Safe Space / "LAM Buffet Table" (existed with Dad but not with grandmother and brother)

+

LAM Energy Work / "Plate" at LAM Buffet

+

Traditional Modalities- parachute play, ball games

+

Non-Traditional Modalities- guided visualization/pretend play, breath work (three part breath), yoga movement, partner yoga, Mantra training ("I can do it").

=

Improved attention/compliance, reduced impulsivity, improved transitioning, greater bonding between dad and son, and improved empathy with grandmother (Limitless Possibilities).

CASE STUDY NUMBER 10:
ED K. AND JAMES

Ed K. was a six-year-old boy referred to the LAM program by the director of the Creative Arts Therapy Center. He lived with both of his parents and a younger sibling. He was diagnosed with Regressive Autism at age three years, one month. Since that time, he had received Early Intervention for ten hours a week. He was attending a specialized school where he received Occupational Therapy 2x/week, Speech Therapy 4x/week, and Applied Behavioral Analysis (ABA) 5x/week. His overall health was reported to be good with seasonal allergies at age five. Ed. K. exhibited hypotonia in his upper extremities and back but didn't qualify for physical therapy. He could express his wants/needs since age four-and-a-half using one or two words and sometimes three word phrases. His parents reported that his receptive language skills were much better than his expressive language. The practitioners also noted that Ed would scream, hit and push when triggered by being told "no." Also, when he encountered new situations and when certain visual, auditory and tactile stimuli were presented in the session room, his negative behaviors would manifest. At home and during LAM sessions, he would engage in parallel play but mostly exhibited a form of solitary rigid play that focused only on the discriminate manipulation of objects in a consistent repeated pattern (i.e. turning a block over and over again in the same manner). The mom was present during the Intake and the dad participated in all eight sessions. Mom did attend one Mindfulness Curriculum Workshop after her son and husband had attended six LAM sessions. Dad never attended any of our Mindfulness Curriculum Workshops.

Both parents accompanied Ed to the first LAM session. However, Ed's mom quickly left the session room and waited outside. During that initial session, Ed was compliant but exhibited lethargy for any task that was presented. He was difficult to engage and his eye contact was poor. He readily accepted the LAM Energy work that increased his overall energy level. The LAM practitioners used the traditional modality of discriminate play with blocks. When he did engage sporadically with the LAM practitioners, he followed some simple 1-step commands such as "Give me" and he spontaneously used some single words. He exhibited perseveration in his discriminate play skills by turning the blocks over and over in the same direction in his hands.

During sessions two to four, there was an inconsistent level of progress observed in various developmental areas. During session two, the LAM practitioners introduced the non-traditional modality of guided visualization/pretend play. Ed exhibited empathy when he hugged an oversized teddy bear. During session three, he exhibited negative behaviors of scratching and biting when it was time to clean up. The LAM practitioners realized that Ed required the creation of a formal safe space during session four. They physically marked out a personal area for Ed with tape. When Ed was alone in this clearly marked physical safe space, improvements were observed in his verbal output, vocal volume, and empathy (e.g. gave father a hug). It was interesting to note that Ed didn't allow his father to enter his personal space during that session but did allow the LAM practitioners to enter.

During sessions four to eight, Ed's discriminate play skills improved with less perseveration (e.g. stacked six to eight blocks). In addition, he manifested other improvements in the following areas: ability to follow 1-step commands, verbal output (e.g. said "hyena" to describe his favorite book, "Good-bye gorilla"), pretend play skills and receptive and expressive language skills. His use of language increased for requesting desired actions from adults. He told his dad, "I want airplane ride." The only LAM non-traditional modality that was introduced was guided visualization/pretend play. Due to his reduced level of cognition and language ability, other non-traditional modalities were unable to be introduced. Even LAM's kangaroo breath could not be taught due to Ed's hypersensitivity to tactile stimuli. LAM energy work was used in conjunction with all modalities.

In conclusion, Ed made moderate progress in the LAM program. At the time of this writing, the LAM practitioners have lost touch with this family and do not know how Ed is progressing.

Summary of the Lesson Plan for Ed K.:

Creation of Safe Space / "LAM Buffet Table" (physically marking out the "safe space" area with tape)

+

LAM Energy Work / "Plate" at LAM Buffet

+

Traditional Modalities- play therapy (discriminate play with blocks), speech therapy (following 1-step directions, increasing verbal output)

+

Non-Traditional Modality- guided visualization/pretend play with stuffed animals

=

Improved empathy, improved transitioning, improved pretend play, reduced perseveration, improved receptive/expressive language skills (Limitless Possibilities).

Parents and professionals, now that you have read the LAM Lesson Plans, it's time to start attending the "LAM Buffet" on your own. There is no right or wrong. Follow your heart and listen to its messages. You will know what to do for the particular child. It may be a whisper, so listen very carefully. LAM believes that less is more and that love and compassion rather than anger and force are the means to move forward with the child in a supportive manner. A playful manner creates the necessary safe space for you and the child to engage positively. The child's progress is not a reflection of your own abilities. Try to keep your distance and be the "observer" rather than the "reactor." In this way, you will support the child on his/her journey rather than trying to fix him/her. We believe that everyone is a mirror for each other. The life lessons you are learning while undertaking the challenging journey of being a parent or a professional of a child with special needs are necessary for your own life's journey. As Tim Shriver, Chairman of the Special Olympics, states in his book *Fully Alive* about his own personal journey, "…we are all totally vulnerable and totally valuable at the same time… I discovered a new way of seeing individuals whom I thought of as 'powerless' but who turned out to have a power I didn't even know existed."[57]

Just as you are all on your own individual journeys, as creators of the LAM program so are we. Come join us on our mutual journey as we explore together LAM's Vision and Hope for the future.

Chapter 8

LAM'S Vision And Hope For The Future

LAM'S VISION:
" Look at the child with special needs and envision the limitless possibilities not the limitations."

FOR PARENTS:

Change Your Paradigm From Fixing to Supporting Your Child With Special Needs.

"Be the change that you want to see in the world (Gandhi)."[58]

Traditionally, all parents expect that their child is going to be a magnificent reflection of all that is valued by society (i.e. beauty, intelligence, talent, etc.).

As parents, when you have a child with special needs who doesn't emanate these societal values and doesn't reflect well on you, everything breaks down. You feel like a "victim." Common emotions that are typically manifested are fear, hurt, abandonment, anger, betrayal, shame, and guilt. "What did I do to deserve this happening to me?" is a common unspoken question you may say to yourself. When you observe other "typically" developing children at play-dates, schools, playgrounds, or daycare centers, and are told how your child is not keeping up with the rest of the group or is misbehaving and causing chaos, you feel enormous responsibility and shame. You feel abandoned and ostracized by the lack of support you are receiving. Instead, you are told to leave or correct your child in some way in order to make the child fit in. This is analogous to trying to fit a square peg into a round hole. It doesn't work! Every parent knows this to be the truth. This truth resides in the deepest part of his/her heart.

A perfect storm is created for these parents when they birth or adopt a child with special needs. It is not uncommon for this population to feel this way because the stress of parenting a child with special needs is enormous! The physical, financial, and emotional toll of parenting a child with special needs cannot be understated. So, why do we as a society keep propagating this parenting paradigm of trying to fix the child into some predetermined pattern in order for that child to be successful in life? To reiterate, Albert Einstein once said, "Insanity is doing the same thing over and over again and expecting different results."[59] If we want to create a different result, then we need to do something DIFFERENT.

That is precisely why the LAM program was created. We as LAM practitioners working with children with special needs realized that a new integrative approach could yield better outcomes for the parent, child and professional. This was the impetus for the creation of the LAM program. "Love, Acceptance, Matters" became the cornerstone and slogan of the LAM program. Every child is deserving of love and acceptance no matter what.

Children with special needs require more love and acceptance than any other group of human beings. Like all children, children with special needs are born innocent, vulnerable and completely open. However, children with special needs do exhibit certain differences in their development. Instead of seeing the unlimited potential of each and every one of these children with special needs, parents tend to view these differences as "defects" that need to be fixed instead of as "opportunities" for growth and support. These children are different not defective. The "differences" exhibited in nature illustrate that "differences" are not "defects." Nature is our biggest teacher.

The variety in nature displays all different possibilities and growing conditions. Some plants like weeds will grow no matter what the growing conditions might be. However, some plants such as orchids require very special growing conditions in order to reach their full potential. Children with special needs are *orchids*. It's important to understand this very simple process from nature. It is easier to grow a weed than it is an *orchid*. Parents of children with special needs have the unique challenge of growing *orchids*.

The results of LAM's *orchid* population have been based on a sample of a wide variety of different developmental and neurological challenges. A sampling of these diagnosed challenges were the following: Down Syndrome, Asperger's Syndrome, Autism Spectrum Disorder, Sensory Processing Disorder, Language Delays, Attention Deficit Hyperactivity Disorder/Attention Deficit Disorder and other genetic abnormalities. In every instance, however, we noticed a particular pattern: the greater the hope and positive outlook of the parent, the more developmental gains the child accomplished during our LAM sessions.

As Sri Swami Satchitananda, a revered Yoga master and spiritual teacher of our time so aptly states, "There is always a positive way of looking at things."[60] Within a very short time, we at LAM realized that it was imperative to change the parents' negative way of thinking about their own issues into a more positive one. This was no easy task. Most parents came to us with their own unresolved emotional baggage and displayed anxiety, depression, low self-esteem, and unresolved family issues. These parents needed nurturing and support as much as their children. At LAM, this was provided during Mindfulness Curriculum Workshops and during their children's sessions. In addition, LAM also offered private LAM sessions to the parents. Most of our parents took advantage of this offering. They started to shift their negative outlook to a more positive one. This created a ripple effect in their families.

During our LAM sessions, parents began to express and release most of their negative emotions since they felt unconditional love and acceptance from the LAM practitioners. This occurrence was nothing short of miraculous and resulted in tremendous inner transformation for some of our parents. The energy transfer between these parents and their children became much more positive. Instead of forcing their child to perform in a certain manner in order to meet preconceived developmental and societal expectations, these parents relaxed and became detached from any particular outcome. Their children reaped the benefits of their parents' courage to surrender and detach from the outcome. Everyone stayed fully present in the moment and didn't worry about the past or future. In the LAM sessions, all participants became united in love and bathed in acceptance. No questions were asked. No judgments were given. This was truly remarkable. Could love and acceptance be the "key" that would unlock the door to "limitless possibilities?" We at LAM think so!

For parents, this transformational process isn't easy. It requires an inordinate amount of courage, patience, and persistence to participate in the LAM program. Even though at any moment children with special needs can act in a manner that is inconsistent with what society deems "appropriate", it is imperative for parents to maintain the neutral stance of being the "observer" vs. the "reactor." It is very easy to fall back into the old negative habitual patterns of shame, grief, guilt and anger. Just like maintaining a new and healthy diet takes mindfulness and perseverance until it becomes a habit, the LAM program requires the same amount of effort. But, it is so worth it!

The most important thing to remember as a parent is to **play with your child**. This is the essential ingredient of every *tool* that is used in the "LAM Virtual Toolbox." It is the way into any child's world and is the essential ingredient for creating a positive and supportive relationship between you and your child. Play creates the safe space which is the "table" at the LAM Buffet.

One of the first *homework assignments* at LAM was for the parent to find the time to play with his/her child uninterrupted for twenty to thirty minutes per day even if the child seemed unresponsive. LAM emphasized how important it was to stay present with the child no matter what in order to allow the free flow of a positive exchange to occur. At the beginning, many parents reported that the *play homework* was really difficult. We instructed our parents to persist and smile and not be their child's *teacher*. We encouraged parents to enjoy the interaction as much as possible with very little judgment. Eventually, the play became more and more of a relational spontaneous exchange. After the first few play sessions, parents started to report how much *fun* they were having with their child and seemed surprised at the emerging feedback they were now receiving from their child. They reported with joy that their child was reacting in a more heart-felt way displaying more appropriate eye contact, joint attention and turn-taking skills. Some of our non-verbal children initially even began pointing and vocalizing spontaneously to express their wants and needs. Other children were even starting to use some single word approximations to comment to their parents. Everyone was so happy when this occurred!

Parents don't be afraid to seek help. Ask for what you and your child both need. Without the proper loving support and compassion from others including and not limited to extended family, friends, and professionals, the new LAM parenting system may falter. Give it time. If it doesn't work initially, be patient and persist. Remember, it takes a *village* to raise a child and it takes a *city* to raise a child with special needs. As Sonia Sumar, founder of Yoga for the Special Child Method, so eloquently states in her book, *Yoga for the Special Child* (p. ix: December 1996):

"During my twenty-three years as a yoga teacher of children with special needs, I have seen many so-called 'hopeless cases' respond to the stimulus of a properly designed remedial yoga program. **However, there first needs to be a strong conviction on the parents' part that their child has the potential to improve**. Sometimes this may seem difficult, especially in the face of opposition and prejudice, but it is an **essential ingredient to the success** of the program. **By letting go of our fears and negativity, and learning to see the best in ourselves and others, we can provide a powerful impetus for positive change.** It is through this ability to **go beyond preconceived notions and external appearances that we can transform our lives and those of our children**. May all the parents of children with special needs develop this ability, and may they and their children experience true peace and happiness."[61]

In conclusion, LAM believes that the success of parenting a child with special needs can be moved forward to the next level by adding the strategies of the "LAM Buffet":

The LAM Buffet

Creation of a Safe Space

+

LAM Energy Work

+

Traditional Modalities

+

Non-traditional Modalities

=

Limitless Possibilities

FOR PROFESSIONALS

Change Your Paradigm From Fixing to Supporting The Child With Special Needs.

"Be the change that you want to see in the world (Gandhi)."[62]

For the professionals who work with this special population of children, the LAM paradigm offers you a more expansive way of envisioning the limitless possibilities for these children. LAM understands the burdens that may obscure your optimism and focus when working with these children. The case history and the diagnostic criteria that are presented to you may limit your ability to perceive the child's hidden potential. Your professional training and expertise, paperwork, and insurance demands may adversely affect your individual perception of the child. Even your own preconceived beliefs about what constitutes a successful outcome may have to shift when this limits your ability to love and accept the child as is. Your own understanding of your professional role has to expand to include this LAM paradigm of supporting rather than fixing. We at LAM urge you to open your mind and heart and view each child in your workplace with limitless possibilities. We urge you to see beyond *symptoms* or *behaviors* and view the child in his/her entirety. Be present and supportive to both the child and the family. All of your positive energy gets transferred subconsciously to both the child and his/her family members. You play a very important role in implementing this LAM paradigm and facilitating the shift in perception from fixing to supporting the child on his/her journey in achieving limitless possibilities. Remember that you are part of the *city* that it takes to raise a child with special needs.

LAM encourages you to shift your perception from a *fixing* and *doing* stance to a *guiding* and *supporting* stance with each and every child while using your expertise combined with the LAM Buffet. Although it is standard protocol to look closely at the child's family structure, family belief patterns, parenting style as well as the child's overall mental, emotional, and physical health during the intake or assessment process, we at LAM are encouraging you to delve deeper into this information using your intuition and heart. Your role now as the professional under this new LAM paradigm would be to see the child in front of you as perfect, whole and complete just as he/she is. You will no longer be *fixing* the child but rather *guiding* or *coaching*. *Fixing* suggests that something about this child is *broken*. *Guiding* or *coaching* suggests that this child has *challenges* and needs *support*. *Fixing* has a negative energetic component while *guiding* or *coaching* has a positive energetic component. This can be described by using nature as a reference.

If one plants a seed in the earth and puts a rock on top of the seed, the seed can't grow. Do you think the seed is broken and needs *fixing*? Or does the seed need someone to move the rock so that the seed can grow? At LAM, we believe that the *seed* represents the child that is perfect and whole just the way he/she is. The rock represents the child's *challenge* or *obstacle*. It is the professional's role to support the seed or child by moving the rock. In that manner, the *seed* or *child* can flourish and grow to his/her full potential.

As any professional knows, one must not underestimate the importance of the role parents do play in the therapeutic process. LAM carries this principle a step further by involving the parent in every session to mirror the LAM practitioner. It is easy to apply this concept when using the "LAM Buffet." We urge you to try to use parents as a tremendous resource whenever possible in your therapeutic practice.

Any therapeutic discipline can use the "LAM BUFFET." We at LAM understand that traditional Western professionals are methodically taught in the standards of their own particular discipline. Professionals must adhere to strict standards of ethical practice. This is all good. However, LAM recommends adding other dimensions to one's therapeutic practice in order to achieve even greater outcomes. The most important dimension is to create the safe space of unconditional love and acceptance between the professional and child. Without this trust, the child can't connect with the professional in a positive manner. Once the safe space is created and trust develops, the traditional therapeutic process of one's particular discipline can begin.

One now has the option of adding any one of the holistic non-traditional modalities offered at the LAM Buffet that has been described in detail in Chapter 5. During this whole process, we at LAM encourage all professionals to transmit to the child and the parent the intention of *guiding* and *supporting*. This will provide the necessary energetic component of a positive exchange between the professional, the parent and the child. We at LAM believe that if a child or parent feels or senses the energy of being broken and needing fixing, this will lead to the development of negative emotions particularly sadness and low self-esteem. However, if the parent and child feel loved, supported and accepted, then the positive emotions of joy and happiness will be evident raising both the parent's and child's self-esteem. Although this phenomenon is not evidence-based, we at LAM believe it has enormous value in creating the right energetic environment for the therapeutic process to be the most effective.

In conclusion, even though specific goals and objectives need to be stated and followed, LAM believes it is important for every professional working with children with special needs to expand their perceived expectations and envision unimagined outcomes. In other words, LAM's Vision for professionals urges you to see the *Forest-The LAM Buffet* and not just the *Trees – Your Specific Professional Discipline*.

The LAM Buffet

Creation of a Safe Space
+
LAM Energy Work
+
Traditional Modalities
+
Non-traditional Modalities
=
Limitless Possibilities

LAM's HOPE

LAM's ABC's

ACCEPTANCE OF LIMITLESS POSSIBILITIES **B**ECOMES **C**OMMONPLACE.

"*Man often becomes what he believes himself to be. If I keep on saying to myself that I cannot do a certain thing, it is possible that I may end by really becoming incapable of doing it. On the contrary, if I have the belief that I can do it, I shall surely acquire the capacity to do it even if I may not have it at the beginning*" (Gandhi)." [63]

A New Journey for Children with Special Needs

According to LAM and holistic wisdom traditions, every child is born whole, perfect and complete regardless of external circumstances. We at LAM believe that all children are born with the fundamental birthright to be loved and accepted unconditionally. When a child is born with special needs, that child lacks the conscious awareness to perceive his/her being as *flawed*. It is society's perception and cultural conditioning that these *flaws* need *fixing* in order for this child to become complete and function successfully in society. As the child grows up, most of the surrounding adults in that child's world express this underlying belief system that this child is *flawed* in some way. They transmit this underlying belief system to the child energetically, verbally and physically. The child's belief system eventually changes. He/she begins to believe in his/her own *flawed* differences and becomes acutely aware of these challenges or *flaws*. These *flaws* are heightened obscuring any other qualities that this child may possess and become his/her self-fulfilling prophecy that says "I can't do it!" These children feel that they are *outsiders, outcasts* and *unacceptable* members of society. Feeling frustrated, unaccepted and unloved, they act out negatively when the frustration becomes unbearable. It is a vicious cycle that needs to be changed.

As Wayne Dyer, PhD, internationally renowned author and speaker in the field of self-development has stated, "If you change the way you look at things, the things you look at change...Deficiency motivation doesn't work. It will lead to a life-long pursuit of try to fix me. Learn to appreciate what you have and where and who you are."[64]

In the LAM program, a new journey for the child with special needs begins with self-acceptance. The LAM program does this by meeting each child exactly where he/she is and offering unconditional love and acceptance. This creates the safe space or the "table" at the LAM Buffet. It is the cornerstone of our LAM program as previously stated. Instead of viewing the child's *differences* as *flaws* that need *fixing*, the LAM practitioners *support* the child and view these *obstacles* as *opportunities* for growth and expansion. When the child begins to relax and have fun because he/she is completely supported and loved, then new positive outcomes are possible and negative behaviors decrease. LAM transmits the energy that "you are OK just the way you are." This doesn't mean that the LAM sessions are completely unstructured and have no particular goals and objectives. Instead, there is a very structured framework to each and every LAM session. However, a flow occurs where the child simply becomes a willing participant and moves forward effortlessly.

After the completion of the LAM program, it is our hope that parents and professionals will view children with special needs as perfect, whole and complete as they are. This phenomenon of a transformational shift will occur in the child, parent and professional. From the child's perspective, the child will no longer define himself/herself by his/her limitations or challenges anymore. Instead, the child would welcome these *challenges* as *opportunities* for growth and expansion.

In the large scheme of things, the child with special needs may even view these challenges as negligible. As so succinctly stated by the main character, Christopher Boone, in the book, "The Curious Incident of the Dog in the Night-Time":

> "When you look at the sky you know you are looking at stars which are hundreds and thousands of light-years away from you. And some of the stars don't even exist anymore because their light has taken so long to get to us that they are already dead, or they have exploded and collapsed into red dwarfs. And that makes you seem very small, and if you have difficult things in your life it is nice to think that they are what is called negligible, which means they are so small you don't have to take them into account when you are calculating something"[65] (protagonist Christopher Boone, age 15, child with special needs)".

We all must never forget that these children are our *orchids* requiring special conditions to grow beautifully. Once these children are given the opportunity to believe in themselves, they enjoy the freedom to grow and expand. They provide us with a more expansive view of the world that can be witnessed by all who are in their presence. Our society views the world from the outside in where a person is defined by his/her outward success or status. Instead, these *orchids* view the world from the inside out. They become our greatest *teachers* through their example. They teach us to look inside the packaging and discover the hidden gems underneath the surface. As so eloquently stated by Tim Shriver in his book, *Fully Alive*:

> "People with intellectual disabilities are brilliant teachers of that something bigger we're all looking for... the breakthrough lesson that all life is beautiful...the athletes of the Special Olympics taught me more about

> how to see than what to see...There's another way of seeing: from the inside out...the great Sufi mystic Rumi suggests that such a way of seeing creates a consciousness that enables us to see possibilities and realities that might otherwise be hidden: The intellect says: 'The six directions are limits: there is no way out. Love says: There is a way. I have traveled it thousands of times."[66]

In conclusion, our goal for the future for children with special needs is to feel unconditional love and acceptance by all human beings from birth to death. Isn't this what everyone wants? LAM believes that if this occurs, these children will grow and develop into beautiful *orchids* with limitless possibilities. In other words, from their very first day here on earth, they will experience what the Buddha calls, "the gladdened heart." If we can invite an attitude of gratitude for these children, then we will be able to understand that that they can teach us how to live from the inside out opening our hearts in the process. Our hope is that LAM's "ABC's": "Acceptance of Limitless Possibilities Becomes Commonplace" will become the new reality for these children.

> Everyone wants to feel content, safe and welcomed in one's life- what Buddha called the "gladdening of the heart." When our awareness and perception change to invite the attitude of appreciation and gratitude in our lives, we experience gratitude no matter how dire the external circumstances. [67]

Moving LAM's Program into the World

Here at LAM, we believe passionately in the efficacy and innovativeness of the LAM program. The LAM Program deserves to become global. Its impact on children with special needs and their families, educators, therapists, and medical professionals will be enormous! How does LAM hope to accomplish this?

It is our hope that parents/grandparents/caregivers of children with special needs will try some of the strategies offered in this book and realize their efficacy. As the paradigm shifts from fixing to supporting the child with special needs, you will be encouraged to explore more techniques to handle more challenging behavioral situations in a new way. We want you to use this book as a "handbook" to guide you along your journey.

Second, we urge passionate professionals who simply love children and want to see all children flourish to try some of the techniques offered in this book. We understand that you as professionals all come from many different disciplines such as integrative medicine, therapy, healthcare and education. It is our hope that this book will offer you additional "tools."

We urge both parents and professionals to be creative risk takers. We hope that you won't accept the status quo that all existing programs out there are the best and are willing to take the leap of faith. The LAM program speaks to the depths of everyone's hearts that we are all deserving of love and acceptance. Please give it a try.

Lastly, we believe that the LAM program is so effective because it aligns with nature. As Deepak Chopra so eloquently states in his 21 day meditation experience entitled "Manifesting Grace through Gratitude" on Day 11- Nature's Generosity is Waiting: "We learn that Nature is always ready to give to us and support us. We only need to open ourselves to that infinite abundance and connect with it."[68] Here at LAM, we teach parents, children and professionals how to connect and align with nature so that they too can experience its generosity, abundance and infinite wisdom.

It is LAM's hope for the future that this connection to one's own authentic self will align with the magnificence of Mother Nature. Mother Nature teaches us that permanence and change can occur simultaneously. For example, weather is unpredictable. However, what is predictable is that there is always a sun shining above the clouds. If we can all accept the unpredictability of living and raising a child with special needs and realize that a light always shines within each and every one of us, then, we can always move towards that permanent light. We at LAM see the rainbow. Can you see it?

A CALL TO ACTION

Are you a creative risk taker? If so, here is your opportunity to be called into action and join the LAM family. In order to do this, please email us and check out our website at www.lamhealingarts.com for more information about upcoming events. LAM looks forward to meeting, talking and supporting your parenting or professional journey.

Chapter 9

LAM's Offering of Inspirational Poems/Quotes/Affirmations

We know at LAM that there is a "rainbow in every cloud"[69] as Maya Angelou so brilliantly said (OWN MASTER CLASS, YouTube). It is LAM's loving offering to provide you with the necessary sustenance, strength and support for those times when the dark clouds seem overwhelming with no hint of a rainbow in sight. Our hope is that this chapter helps you see rainbows each and every day whether it is cloudy or sunny.

Intention

"No one undertakes research in physics with the intention of winning a prize. It is the joy of discovering something no one knew before." [70]

– Stephen Hawking

"Limitations live only in our minds. But, if we use our imaginations, our possibilities become limitless."[71]

- Jamie Paolinetti, former domestic American professional cyclist and previous national champion

"The mind is everything. What you think you become."[72]

– Buddha

"The most common way people give up their power is by thinking they don't have any."[73]

– Alice Walker, author of *The Color Purple*.

" When I let go of what I am, I become what I might be."[74]

– Lao Tzu

"The only person you are destined to become is the person you decide to be." [75]

- Ralph Waldo Emerson

"One of the hardest things to do as a parent is to allow our children to be who they want to be."[76]

-Madisyn Taylor, best-selling author and editor-in-chief of DailyOM

"You were born with potential.
You were born with goodness and trust.
You were born with ideals and dreams.
You were born with greatness.
You were born with wings.
You are not meant for crawling, so don't.
You have wings.
Learn to use them and fly." [77]

-Rumi

"See the miraculous in everything."[78]

– Dr. Wayne W. Dyer

"There are only two ways to live your life. One is as though nothing is a miracle. The other is as though everything is a miracle." [79]

- Albert Einstein

"Start by doing what's necessary; then do what's possible; and suddenly you are doing the impossible." [80]

–St. Francis of Assisi

"Never say never. Always say 'I can' and 'I will.'"[81]

-Lois A. Mettler
(co-founder/co-creator of LAM Healing Arts, LLC.)

"When you believe in yourself, anything is possible!" [82]

-Adrienne L. Murphy
(co-founder/co-creator of LAM Healing Arts, LLC.)

Courage

"It is not the critic who counts; not the man who points out how the strong man stumbles, or where the doer of deeds could have done them better. The credit belongs to the man who is actually in the arena, whose face is marred by dust and sweat and blood; who strives valiantly; who errs, who comes short again and again, because there is no effort without error and shortcoming; but who does actually strive to do the deeds; who knows great enthusiasms, the great devotions; who spends himself in a worthy cause; who at the best knows in the end the triumph of high achievement, and who at the worst, if he fails, at least fails while daring greatly, so that his place shall never be with those cold and timid souls who neither know victory nor defeat." [83]

-Theodore Roosevelt

"Let me win, but if I cannot win, let me be brave in the attempt." [84]

- Special Olympics Oath

Origin of the Special Olympics Athlete Oath:

"In ancient Rome, the gladiators went into the arena with these words on their lips: Let me win, but if I cannot win, let me be brave in the attempt. Today, all of you young athletes are in the arena. Many of you will win, but even more important, I know you will be brave, and bring credit to your parents and to your country. Let us begin the Olympics. Thank you."[85]

- Eunice Kennedy Shriver, Special Olympics Founder
- International Special Olympics Summer Games in 1968 at Soldier Field, Chicago, Illinois, USA, with a personal pledge to give all individuals with intellectual disabilities a chance to compete and a chance to grow.

"Your living is determined not so much by what life brings to you as by the attitude you bring to life; not so much by what happens to you as by the way your mind looks at what happens. Circumstances and situations do color life, but you have been given the mind to choose what the color will be."[86]

– John Homer Miller

"We must be willing to get rid of the life we've planned, so as to have the life that is awaiting us."[87]

- Joseph Campbell

"Where there is darkness, let me bring light…"[88]

-St. Francis of Assisi

"Everything has beauty, but not everyone sees it ."[89]

– Confucious

"It does not matter how slowly you go as long as you do not stop."[90]

–Confucious

"To love ourselves and support each other in the process of becoming real is perhaps the greatest single act of daring greatly." [91]

–Brene Brown

"Only when we're brave enough to explore the darkness will we discover the infinite power of our light."[92]

– Brene Brown

"As I look back on what I've learned about shame, gender, and worthiness, the greatest lesson is this: If we're going to find our way out of shame and back to each other, vulnerability is the path and courage is the light. To set down those lists of what we're supposed to be is brave. To love ourselves and support each other in the process of becoming real is perhaps the greatest single act of daring greatly." [93]

– Brene Brown

"The only thing we have to fear is fear itself…" [94]

– Franklin D. Roosevelt

Trust

"Parenting asks us to rise to some of the most difficult challenges this world has to offer, and one of its greatest paradoxes arises around the issue of attachment. On the one hand, successful parenting requires that we love our children, and most of us love in a very attached way. On the other hand, it also requires that we let go of our children at the appropriate times, which means we must practice some level of nonattachment. Many parents find this difficult because we love our children fiercely, more than we will ever love anyone, and this can cause us to overstep our bounds with them as their independence grows. Yet truly loving them requires that we set them free.

Letting go in any area of life requires a deep trust in the universe, in the overall meaning and purpose of existence. Remembering that there is more to us and our children than meets the eye can help us practice nonattachment, even when we feel overwhelmed by concern and the desire to interfere. We are all souls making our way in the world and making our way, ultimately, back to the same source. This can be our mantra as we let our children go in peace and confidence."[95]

- Madisyn Taylor, best-selling author and editor-in-chief of DailyOM.

"Few things can help an individual more than to place responsibility on him, and to let him know that you trust him."[96]

– Booker T. Washington

"When one door of happiness closes, another opens, but often we look so long at the closed door that we do not see the one that has been opened for us."[97]

– Helen Keller

"It is not what you do for your children, but what you have taught them to do for themselves, that will make them successful human beings."[98]

- Ann Landers

"There are as many opinions as there are experts." [99]

– Franklin D. Roosevelt

"If you have total faith in a Higher Will- a Higher Energy- you will be able to tune in to that and receive all the strength and energy to recharge your system."[100]

– Sri Swami Satchidananda, One of the first yoga masters to bring classical yoga tradition to the West.

Compassion

I am the child who cannot talk.
You often pity me, I see it in your eyes.
You wonder how much I am aware of – I see that as well.
I am aware of much-whether you are happy or sad or fearful,
Patient or impatient, full of love and desire,
Or if you are just doing your duty by me.
I marvel at your frustration, knowing mine to be far greater,
For I cannot express myself or my needs as you do.

You cannot conceive my isolation, so complete it is at times.
I do not gift you with clever conversation, cute remarks to be laughed over and repeated.
I do not give you answers to your everyday questions, responses over my well-being, sharing my needs, or comments about the world about me.
I do not give you rewards as defined by the world's standards-
Great strides in development that you can credit yourself.
I do not give you understanding as you know it.

What I give you is so much more valuable- I give instead opportunities.
Opportunities to discover the depth of your character, not mine;
The depth of your love, your commitment, your patience, your abilities:
The opportunity to explore your spirit more deeply than you imagined possible.
I drive you further than you would ever go on your own,
Working harder, seeking answers to your many questions with no answers.
I am the child who cannot talk.
I am the child who cannot walk.
The world seems to pass me by.
You see the longing in my eyes to get out of this chair,
To run and play like other children.
There is much you take for granted.
I want the toys on the shelf, I need to go to the bathroom, oh I've dropped my fork again.
I am dependent on you in these ways.

My gift to you is to make you more aware of your great fortune,
Your healthy back and legs, your ability to do for yourself.
Sometimes people appear not to notice me; I always notice them.
I feel not so much envy as desire, desire to stand upright,
To put one foot in front of the other, to be independent.
I give you awareness.
I am the child who cannot walk.

I am the child who is mentally impaired.
I don't learn easily, if you judge me by the world's measuring stick, what I do know is infinite joy in simple things.
I am not burdened as you are with the strifes and conflicts of a more complicated life.
My gift to you is to grant you the freedom to enjoy things as a child,
To teach you how much your arms around me mean,
To give you love.
I give you the gift of simplicity.
I am the child who is mentally impaired.
I am the disabled child.
I am your teacher.
If you allow me, I will teach you what is really important in life.
I will give and teach you unconditional love.
I gift you with my innocent trust, my dependency upon you.
I teach you about how precious this life is and about not taking things for granted.
I teach you about forgetting your own needs and desires and dreams.
I teach you giving.
Most of all, I teach you hope and faith.
I am the disabled child.[101]

-Author Unknown

Blessing for a Child

"Dear precious child of God,
Beautiful one,

Sweet unfolding blossom,
I give you my deepest blessing
My fondest wish,
For a wonderful, magical life,
Filled with love, happiness,
Adventure, fulfillment, serenity,
Beauty and health.
I love you and God loves you.
May you know this with all the strength of your being.
May you be free." [102]

- Mary Sigman

Love

"Real love is possible only when you see everything as an expression of yourself. It has no boundaries; it is the greatest force on earth.

The whole world exists in love. We come with love and we go with love.

And, in between, we live with love. Love is the basis of everything." [103]
- Sri Swami Satchidananda, One of the first yoga masters to bring classical yoga tradition to the West.

"Truth and love have always won."[104]

– Gandhi

"The most terrible poverty is loneliness and the feeling of being unloved."

"If you judge people, you have no time to love them."

"Every time you smile at someone, it is an action of love, a gift to that person, beautiful thing."

"Kind words can be short and easy to speak, but their echoes are truly endless."

"Not all of us can do great things. But we can do small things with great love."

"The hunger for love is much more difficult to remove than the hunger for bread."

"I can do things you cannot, you can do things I cannot; together we can do great things." [105]

– Mother Theresa

"Love is the ability and willingness to allow those that you care for to be what they choose for themselves without any insistence that they satisfy you." [106]

- Wayne Dyer

Gratitude

"One looks back with appreciation to the brilliant teachers, but with gratitude to those who touched our human feelings. The curriculum is so much necessary raw material, but warmth is the vital element for the growing plant and for the soul of the child." [107]

– Carl Jung

"The more you are grateful for what you have, the more you can live fully in the present."[108]

-Dana Arcuri

"It is through gratitude for the present moment that the spiritual dimension of life opens up." [109]

– Eckhart Tolle

"In grace, the heart sings."[110]

– Deepak Chopra

" The way to develop the best that is in a person is by appreciation and encouragement." [111]

– Charles Schwab

"The light of your rainbow, your gratitude and grace can transform any experience for you and you can transform any experience for someone else."[112]

- Oprah Winfrey

"As we express our gratitude, we must never forget that the highest appreciation is not to utter words, but to live by them. "[113]

– John F. Kennedy

Acceptance

"In the infinity of life where I am, all is perfect, whole and complete.
I see any resistance patterns within me only as something else to release.
They have no power over me. I am the power in my world.
I flow with the changes taking place in my life as best I can.
I approve of myself and the way I am changing.
I am doing the best I can. Each day gets easier.
I rejoice that I am in the rhythm and flow
Of my ever-changing life.
Today is a wonderful day.
I choose to make it so.
All is well in my world." [114]

- Louise Hay

"Life is what happens to you while you're busy making other plans." [115]

– John Lennon

" Start where you are. Use what you have. Do what you can." [116]

– Arthur Ashe

Nature

"I believe in the subtle magnetism in Nature, which, if we unconsciously yield to it, will direct us aright."[117]

-Henry David Thoreau

"Nature is man's teacher. She unfolds her treasures to his search, unseals his eye, illumes his mind, and purifies his heart; an influence breathes from all the sights and sounds of her existence." [118]

- Alfred Billing Street, American author and poet

"Everything in nature contains all the power of nature. Everything is made of one hidden stuff. Adopt the pace of nature. Her secret is patience." [119]

– Ralph Waldo Emerson

"In all things of Nature, there is something of the marvelous." [120]

– Aristotle

"One who lives in accordance with nature, does not go against the way of things. He moves in harmony with the present moment, always knowing the truth of just what to do." [121]

- Dr. Wayne Dyer

Endnotes

1 *"The Whole World exists in love...everything"*. Sri Swami Satchidananda, mobile. twiiter.com, accessed September, 2011.
2 *"Two Large Pots"*, *Chinese Story*, Anonymous Author.
3 *"Be the change you wish...world"*. Gandhi. www.brainyquotes.com.
4 Definition of energy, wwwthefreedictionary.com.
5 Definition of energy, www.teslasociety.com.
6 Hill, Napoleon, *Think and Grow Rich*, (New York: Penguin Group, 2003), p. 196.
7 Hicks, Esther and Jerry, *Money and the Law of Attraction: Learning to Attract Health, Wealth & Happiness*, (New York: Hay House, 2008), p.16.
8 Definition of Newton's Third Law of Motion- The Physics Classroom, www.physicsclassroom.com/class/newtlaws/Lesson-4/Newton-s-Third-Law.
9 Deepak Chopra and Oprah Winfrey- Oprah & Deepak's 21-Day Meditation Experience, Energy of Attraction, Day 1 Meditation.
10 *"A thing...plan"*. www.merriam-webster.com.
11 *"An act ... result"*. www.dictionary.com.
12 Ron Suskind, *Life Animated*, (New York & Los Angeles: Kingswell, 2014), p.2.
13 Ibid. p. 22.
14 Ibid. p. 23.
15 Ibid. p. 24.
16 *"The ego ...judgments"*. Deepak Chopra. www.deepakchopra.com.
17 *"When you live ... compass"*. Dr. Phil. www.drphil.com.
18 *"The authentic self is...do"*. Dr. Phil. www.drphil.com.
19 *"The field of possibilities...power"*. Deepak Chopra. www.deepakchopra.com.
20 Timothy Shriver, *Fully Alive*, (New York: Sarah Crichton Books, 2014), p.8.
21 Ibid. p. 4.
22 *"We can go beyond ego...speech"*. Deepak Chopra. www.deepakchopra.com.
23 Sheryl Edsall, *Naturally Yoga Teacher Training Manual*, 2011, p. 38.
24 Roger Jahnke, *The Healer Within*, (New York: Harper Collins, 1997), p. 3.
25 Louise Hay, *The Power is Within You*, (USA: Hay House Inc., 1991), p.43.
26 Louise Hay, *You Can Heal Your Life*, (Santa Monica, California: Hay House Inc., 1984), p.93.
27 American Academy of Pediatrics. "Media and Children". www.aap.org,.
28 "Learn about Gross Motor Skills Development" by Ann Logsdon, Learning Disabilities Expert. www.learningdisabilities.about.com,
29 "Exercise: An Alternative ADHD Treatment Without Side Effects" by John Rafey, MD. www.additudemag.com
30 "About SPD". spdfoundation.net.
31 "What is a sensory diet?" www. sensorysmarts.com.
32 "The Benefits of Yoga for Children" by Kristin Henningsen, MS, adjunct professor of Kaplan University of Health Sciences, wellness. Kaplan. Edu.
33 "The Benefits of Yoga on the Parasympathetic Nervous System by Eileen Pfefferle, Demand Media.www.healthyliving.azcentral.com.
34 Sonia Sumar. *Yoga for the Special Child*, (Buckingham, VA: Special Yoga Publications, 1998), p.vii.
35 Ibid.pp.69.
36 Ibid. p. 70
37 Ibid. p. 92.
38 Ibid. p. 124.

39 Ibid. p. 125.
40 Ibid. pp. 171-172.
41 Ibid p. 173.
42 Ibid. pp. 223-224.
43 Ibid. p. 225.
44 Helen Purperhart. *The Yoga Adventure for Children,* (California: Hunter House, 2007), p. 58.
45 "Why Synchronize and Bond With Your Children", Darcia Narvaez Ph. D. www.Psychologytoday.com.
46 Helen Purperhart, *The Yoga Adventure For Children,* (California: Hunter House, 2007) pp. 58-59.
47 Roger Jahnke, *The Healer Within,* (New York: Harper Collins, 1997), p. 30.
48 *Ibid,* p. 36.
49 *"If I were not a physicist, I would…music".* Albert Einstein. www.goodreads.com.
50 *"Sound Healing uses the power…voice".* www.ancientechoes.net. Services/ Sound Healing.
51 Masaru Emoto. *The Hidden Messages in Water.* (Hillsboro, Oregon: Beyond Words Publishing, Inc., 2004, p. ix.
52 Oppositional Defiant Disorder definition. www.mayoclinic.org.
53 Oppositional Defiant Disorder symptoms. www.mayoclinic.org.
54 Oppositional Defiant Disorder risk factors. www. mayoclinic.org.
55 Deepak Chopra and Oprah Winfrey- Oprah & Deepak's 21-Day Meditation Experience, Miraculous Relationships, Day 10 Meditation.
56 "The Law of Attraction", https://en.wikipedia.org/wiki/Law_of _attraction(New_ Thought)
57 Timothy Shriver. *Fully Alive.* (New York: Sarah Crichton Books, 2014), pp. 8-9.
58 *"Be the change…world ".* Gandhi. www.brainyquotes.com.
59 *"Insanity…results".* Albert Einstein. www.goodreads.com.
60 Sri Swami Satchidananda. *Gems of Wisdom (Yogaville: Integral Yoga Publications), p. 49.*
61 Sonia Sumar. *Yoga for the Special Child.* (Buckingham, VA: Special Yoga Publications, 1998), p. ix.
62 *"Be the change … world ".* Gandhi. www.brainyquotes.com.
63 *"Man often becomes…beginning".* Gandhi. www.brainyquotes.com.
64 *"If you change… you are ".* Dr. Wayne Dyer, PhD. www.brainyquotes.com.
65 *"When…something".* www.goodreads.com. Excerpted from *The Curious Incident of the Dog in Night-Time* by Mark Haddon.
66 Timothy Shriver. *Fully Alive.* (New York: Sarah Crichton Books, 2014), pp. 8-9.
67 Deepak Chopra and Oprah Winfrey, Oprah & Deepak's 21-Day Meditation Experience, Manifesting Grace through Gratitude Meditation, Day 3 Meditation.
68 Ibid. Day 11 Meditation.
69 *"Rainbow…cloud".* Maya Angelou. OWN Master class. Youtube.com.
70 *"No one…before".* Stephen Hawking. www.brainyquote.com.
71 *"Limitations live…minds".* Jamie Paolinetti.www.goodreads.com.
72 *"The mind …become".* Buddha.www.brainyquotes.com.
73 *The most…any".* Alice Walker. htttps://en.m. wikiquote.org.
74 *"When…be".* LaoTzu. www.goodreads.com.
75 *"The only person…be".* Ralph Waldo Emerson.www.goodreads.com.
76 *"One…be".* Madisyn Taylor. "Allowing Our Children to Be- Practicing Nonattachment", facebook.com, accessed 1/4/13.
77 *"You were…fly".* Rumi. www.goodreads.com.
78 Wayne Dyer. *Change Your Thoughts-Change Your Life* (New York: HayHouse Inc., 2007), p. 341.
79 *"There are…miracle".* Albert Einstein. www.Goodreads.com.

Endnotes

80 *"Start...impossible"*. St. Francis of Assisi. www.brainyquote.com.
81 *"Never...will"*. Lois Mettler, co-creator LAM Program.
82 *"When...possible"*. Adrienne L. Murphy, co-creator LAM Program .
83 *"It is...defeat"*. Theodore Roosevelt. Theodore-roosevelt.com "The Man In the Arena"- excerpt from the speech "Citizenship in a Republic", delivered at the Sorbonne, in Paris, France on April 23, 1910.
84 *"Let me...attempt"*. Somena.org.
85 *"In ancient Rome...thank you"*. Eunice Kennedy Shriver. Somena.org.
86 John Homer Miller. *A Daybook of Positive Thinking, Daily Affirmations of Gratitude and Happiness*, (Colorado: Blue Mountain Arts, Inc., 2011), p.112.
87 *"We must be ...us"*. Joseph Campbell. www. goodreads.com.
88 *"Where there...light"*. St. Francis of Assisi. Blue Mountain Center of Meditation. www.easwaran.org
89 *"Everything...it"*. Confucious. www. positivelypositve.com.
90 *"It does...stop"*. Confucious. www.brainyquote.com.
91 *"To love...greatly"*. Brene Brown. www.goodreads.com.
92 *"Only when...light"*. Brene Brown. www.goodreads.com.
93 *"As I look...greatly"*. Brene Brown. www. goodreads.com.
94 *"The only thing...itself"*. Franklin D. Roosevelt. Teachinghistory.org.
95 *"Parenting...confidence"*. Madisyn Taylor. www.dailyom.com, accessed 3/17/15.
96 *"Few...him"*. Booker T. Washington. www.brainyquote.com.
97 *"When one door...us"*. Helen Keller. www.goodreads.com.
98 *"It is ...human beings"*. Ann Landers. www.goodreads.com.
99 *"There are as many...experts"*. Franklin D. Roosevelt. www.brainyquote.com.
100 Sri Swami Satchidananda. *Gems of Wisdom.* (Yogaville: Integral Yoga Publications), p.18.
101 *"I am the child...child"*. Author Unknown. Oafccd.com.
102 *"Dear precious child...free"*. Mary Sigman.
103 *"Real love...love"*. Sri Swami Satchidananda. www.goodreads.com.
104 *"Truth and love...won"*. Gandhi. www.goodreads.com.
105 *"The most terrible...things"*. Mother Theresa. www.goodreads.com.
106 *"Love is the ability...you"*. Wayne Dyer. www.brainyquote.com.
107 *"One looks back...the child"*. Carl Jung. www.brainyquote.com.
108 *"The more...present"*. Dana Arcuri. www.goodreads.com.
109 *"It is ...opens up"*. Eckhart Tolle. www.brainyquote.com
110 Deepak Chopra and Oprah Winfrey, Oprah & Deepak's 21-Day Meditation Experience, Manifesting Grace through Gratitude Meditation, Day 17 Meditation.
111 *"The way to develop...encouragement"*. Charles Schwab. www.gratitudehabitat.com/gratitude-quotes/.
112 Deepak Chopra and Oprah Winfrey, Oprah & Deepak's 21-Day Meditation Experience, Manifesting Grace through Gratitude Meditation, Centering Thought Day 19 Meditation.
113 *"As we... them"*. John F. Kennedy. www.brainyquote.com
114 Louise Hay. *You Can Heal Your Life.* (Santa Monica, CA: Hay House, 1984), p. 68.
115 *"Life is what...plans"*. John Lennon. www.brainyquote.com
116 *"Start...you can"*. Arthur Ashe. www.brainyquote.com.
117 *"I believe...aright"*. Henry D. Thoreau. www.goodreads.com.
118 *"Nature...existence"*. Alfred Billing Street. gaiaminute.wordpress.com.
119 *"Everything...patience"*. Ralph Waldo Emerson. gaiaminute.wordpress.com.
120 *"In all things...marvelous"*. Aristotle. www.brainyquote.com.
121 Wayne Dyer. *Change Your Thoughts-Change Your Life.* (New York: Hay House, Inc., 2007), p. 40.

Adrienne L. Murphy MA CCC-SLP, RYT-200, Energy Practitioner graduated from Providence College Summa Cum Laude in the Liberal Arts Honors Program with a BA in Humanities/Business Studies in 1988. She received a graduate fellowship to study speech-language pathology at Montclair State University and graduated Summa Cum Laude with an MA in Speech-Language Pathology from Montclair State University in 1995. She received her Certificate of Clinical Competence (CCC) from the American Speech-Language and Hearing Association in 1996. In her twenty years of practice in speech-language pathology, Adrienne has worked with both children and adults in a wide variety of clinical settings- hospitals, nursing homes, rehab facilities and outpatient therapy clinics. Over the past 15 years of practice, she has worked exclusively with children ages 0-3 in Bergen County New Jersey's Early Intervention System and with school-aged children in her private practice. Adrienne is a skilled expert in the areas of Autism and Autism Spectrum Disorders, Dyspraxia, Learning Disabilities, and Oral Motor/Sensory Feeding Disorders. In 2011, Adrienne received her 200 hour Yoga Alliance Certification from Naturally Yoga in Glen Rock, NJ which changed the course of Adrienne's journey both professionally and personally. She went on to obtain additional certifications in energy healing, qigong and sound therapy. At LAM, she integrates all of these healing modalities for nurturing and facilitating each child's skills.

She believes that this brings out the best in every child. "I offer trust, compassion, validation, support and hope for the whole family. This creates peace and a deeper connection to every child. It is my privilege and honor to be of service in this way offering our LAM programs for children with special needs and their parents."

Lois Mettler, MA Science Education 1969, American Council on Exercise Certified Personal Trainer since 2005, Pilates Certified 2007, Yoga Certified 2011, Energy Practitioner, 2012, graduated in 1965 from Hunter College with a BA in Human Physiology/Biology when she was 19 years old and began her high school science teaching career. She received her Masters of Science Education from New York University in 1969. In 1977, she started a performing arts business, "The Peppermint Playhouse Puppeteers," with her sister to bring Ecology and Health messages into nursery, elementary and special needs schools through the vehicle of original, fun-filled, educational, full- stage puppet productions. For over 30 years she performed all over the tri-state metropolitan area in hundreds of schools each year. The business officially closed in 2012. As this transition was occurring, her desire to learn "The Secret to Good Health and Well Being" led her to become an ACE Certified Personal Trainer, a Certified Pilates and Spin Instructor, and a RYT200 hour Yoga Alliance teacher from Naturally Yoga in Glen Rock, NJ. She obtained certifications in energy healing, qigong, and sound therapy. Her motto is "Everyone has the ability to live a peaceful and fun-filled life no matter what the challenges are. They just need the support, love, and guidance to discover their abilities." She feels honored to be able to partner with Adrienne to create the LAM Program for special needs children and their parents so that they can become their best selves and live happy and productive lives.

www.ingramcontent.com/pod-product-compliance
Lightning Source LLC
Chambersburg PA
CBHW070759100426
42742CB00012B/2194